CW01662247

CONFEDERATION OF TOURISM AND HOSPITALITY

The Global Hospitality Industry

Study Guide

THIS STUDY GUIDE

BPP Learning Media is the **official publisher** for the CTH Diplomas in Hotel Management and Tourism Management.

IN THIS MARCH 2010 FIRST EDITION

- The CTH 2009 syllabus, cross-referenced to the chapters
- Comprehensive syllabus coverage, reviewed and approved by CTH
- Plenty of activities, examples and discussion topics to demonstrate and practise technique
- Full index
- A full CTH past exam for exam practice

BPP LEARNING MEDIA

First edition March 2010

ISBN 9780 7517 7703 1

British Library Cataloguing-in-Publication Data
A catalogue record for this book
is available from the British Library

Published by

BPP Learning Media Ltd
BPP House, Aldine Place
London W12 8AA

www.bpp.com/learningmedia

Printed in the United Kingdom

Your learning materials, published by BPP Learning Media Ltd, are printed on paper sourced from sustainable, managed forests.

We are grateful to the Confederation of Tourism and Hospitality for permission to reproduce the syllabus and past examination questions and answers.

We would like to acknowledge the invaluable contribution of Andrew Pennington in the preparation of this Study Guide.

A note about copyright

Dear Customer

What does the little © mean and why does it matter?

Your market-leading BPP books, course materials and e-learning materials do not write and update themselves. People write them: on their own behalf or as employees of an organisation that invests in this activity. Copyright law protects their livelihoods. It does so by creating rights over the use of the content.

Breach of copyright is a form of theft – as well as being a criminal offence in some jurisdictions, it is potentially a serious breach of professional ethics.

With current technology, things might seem a bit hazy but, basically, without the express permission of BPP Learning Media:

- Photocopying our materials is a breach of copyright
- Scanning, ripcasting or conversion of our digital materials into different file formats, uploading them to facebook or e-mailing them to your friends is a breach of copyright

You can, of course, sell your books in the form in which you have bought them – once you have finished with them. (Is this fair to your fellow students? We update for a reason.) But the e-products are sold on a single user licence basis: we do not supply 'unlock' codes to people who have bought them second-hand.

And what about outside the UK? BPP Learning Media strives to make our materials available at prices students can afford by local printing arrangements, pricing policies and partnerships which are clearly listed on our website. A tiny minority ignore this and indulge in criminal activity by illegally photocopying our material or supporting organisations that do. If they act illegally and unethically in one area, can you really trust them?

CONTENTS

How to use this Study Guide

This is the first edition of BPP Learning Media's ground-breaking Study Guide for the *Global Hospitality Industry* paper of the CTH Diploma in Hotel Management. It has been specifically written to cover the syllabus, and has been fully reviewed by CTH.

To pass the examination you need a thorough understanding in all areas covered by the syllabus.

Recommended approach

(a) To pass you need to be able to answer questions on **everything** specified by the syllabus. Read the Study Guide very carefully and do not skip any of it.

(b) Learning is an **active** process. Do **all** the activities as you work through the Study Guide so you can be sure you really understand what you have read.

(c) After you have covered the material in the Study Guide, work through the questions in the practice exam at the back.

(d) Before you take the real exam, check that you still remember the material using the following quick revision plan.

   (i) Read through the chapter learning objectives. Are there any gaps in your knowledge? If so, study the section again.

   (ii) Read and learn the key terms.

   (iii) Read and try to memorise the summary at the end of each chapter.

   (iv) Do the self-test questions again. If you know what you're doing, they shouldn't take long.

This approach is only a suggestion. You or your college may well adapt it to suit your needs.

Remember this is a **practical** course.

(a) Try to relate the material to your experience in the workplace or any other work experience you may have had.

(b) Try to make as many links as you can to other CTH papers that you may be studying at the moment.

Help yourself study for your CTH exams

Exams for professional bodies such as CTH are very different from those you may have taken at school or college. You will be under **greater time pressure** before the exam – as you may be combining your study with work. There are many different ways of learning and so the BPP Learning Media Study Guide offers you a number of different tools to help you through. Here are some hints and tips: they are not plucked out of the air, but **based on research and experience**. (You don't need to know that long-term memory is in the same part of the brain as emotions and feelings – but it's a fact anyway.)

The right approach

1 **The right attitude**

Believe in yourself

Yes, there is a lot to learn. Yes, it is a challenge. But thousands have succeeded before and you can too.

Remember why you're doing it

Studying might seem a grind at times, but you are doing it for a reason: to advance your career.

2 **The right focus**

Read through the syllabus and the chapter objectives

These tell you what you are expected to know.

Study the Exam Paper section

It helps to be familiar with the structure of the exam that you are going to take.

3 **The right method**

The whole picture

You need to grasp the detail – but keeping in mind how everything fits into the whole picture will help you understand better.

- The **objectives and topic list** of each chapter put the material in context.
- The **syllabus content** shows you what you need to **grasp**.

In your own words

To absorb the information (and to practise your written communication skills), it helps to **put it into your own words**.

- **Take notes**.
- Answer the **questions** in each chapter. You will practise your written communication skills, which become increasingly important as you progress through your CTH exams.
- Draw **mindmaps**. The chapter summaries can be a good starting point for this.
- Try **'teaching' a subject** to a colleague or friend.

Give yourself cues to jog your memory

The BPP Study Guide uses **bold** to **highlight key points**.

- Try **colour coding** with a highlighter pen.
- Write **key points** on cards.

4 **The right review**

Review, review, review

It is a **fact** that regularly reviewing a topic in summary form can **fix it in your memory**. Because **review** is so important, the BPP Study Guide helps you to do so in many ways.

- **Chapter summaries** draw together the key points in each chapter. Use them to recap each study session.
- The **self-test questions** are another review technique you can use to ensure that you have grasped the essentials.
- Go through the **examples and illustrations** in each chapter a second or third time.

Developing your personal study plan

BPP's **Learning to Learn Accountancy** book (which can be successfully used by students studying for any professional qualification) emphasises the need to prepare (and use) a study plan. Planning and sticking to the plan are key elements of learning success.

There are four steps you should work through.

STEP 1 **How do you learn?**

First you need to be aware of your style of learning. The BPP Learning Media **Learning to Learn Accountancy** book commits a chapter to this **self-discovery**. What types of intelligence do you display when learning? You might be advised to brush up on certain study skills before launching into this Study Guide.

BPP Learning Media's **Learning to Learn Accountancy** book helps you to identify what intelligences you show more strongly and then details how you can tailor your study process to your preferences. It also includes handy hints on how to develop intelligences you exhibit less strongly, but which might be needed as you study for your professional qualification.

Are you a **theorist** or are you more **practical**? If you would rather get to grips with a theory before trying to apply it in practice, you should follow the study sequence on page (vii). If the reverse is true (you like to know why you are learning theory before you do so), you might be advised to flick through Study Guide chapters and look at examples, case studies and questions (Steps 8, 9 and 10 in the **suggested study sequence**) before reading through the detailed theory.

STEP 2 **How much time do you have?**

Work out the time you have available per week, given the following.

- The standard you have set yourself
- The time you need to set aside later for revision work
- The other exam(s) you are sitting
- Very importantly, practical matters such as work, travel, exercise, sleep and social life

		Hours
Note your time available each week in box A.	A	

STEP 3 **Allocate your time**

▪ Take the time you have available per week for this Study Guide shown in box A, multiply it by the number of weeks available and insert the result in box B.	B	
▪ Divide the figure in box B by the number of chapters in this text and insert the result in box C.	C	

Remember that this is only a rough guide. Some of the chapters in this book are longer and more complicated than others, and you will find some subjects easier to understand than others.

STEP 4 **Implement**

Set about studying each chapter in the time shown in box C, following the key study steps in the order suggested by your particular learning style.

This is your personal **study plan**. You should try and combine it with the study sequence outlined below. You may want to modify the sequence a little (as has been suggested above) to adapt it to your personal **style**.

BPP Learning Media's **Learning to Learn Accountancy** gives further guidance on developing a study plan, and deciding where and when to study.

Suggested study sequence

It is likely that the best way to approach this Study Guide is to tackle the chapters in the order in which you find them. Taking into account your individual learning style, you could follow this sequence.

Key study steps	Activity
Step 1 **Topic list**	Look at the topic list at the start of each chapter. Each topic represents a section in the chapter.
Step 2 **Explanations**	Proceed methodically through the chapter, reading each section thoroughly and making sure you understand.
Step 3 **Definitions**	Definitions can often earn you **easy marks** if you state them clearly and correctly in an appropriate exam answer
Step 4 **Note taking**	Take brief notes, if you wish. Avoid the temptation to copy out too much. Remember that being able to put something into your own words is a sign of being able to understand it. If you find you cannot explain something you have read, read it again before you make the notes.
Step 5 **Examples**	Follow each through to its solution very carefully.
Step 6 **Discussion topics**	Study each one, and try to add flesh to them from your own experience. They are designed to show how the topics you are studying come alive (and often come unstuck) in the real world.
Step 7 **Activities**	Make a very good attempt at each one.
Step 8 **Answers**	Check yours against ours, and make sure you understand any discrepancies.
Step 9 **Chapter summary**	Work through it carefully, to make sure you have grasped the significance of all the key areas.
Step 10 **Self-test questions**	When you are happy that you have covered the chapter, use the self-test questions to check how much you have remembered of the topics covered and to practise questions in a variety of formats.
Step 11 **Question practice**	Either at this point, or later when you are thinking about revising, make a full attempt at the practice exam.

Moving on...

However you study, when you are ready to start your revision, you should still refer back to this Study Guide, both as a source of **reference** (you should find the index particularly helpful for this) and as a way to **review** (the chapter summaries and self-test questions help you here).

And remember to keep careful hold of this Study Guide – you will find it invaluable in your work.

More advice on study skills can be found in BPP Learning Media's **Learning to Learn Accountancy book**.

Syllabus

DIPLOMA PROGRAMMES MODULE SYLLABUS

DHM 192: The Global Hospitality Industry

Description

This module will provide students with an understanding of the hospitality environment, including appreciating the scope of the operations and facilities which shape the hospitality industry. It will investigate the external influences on the industry and consider how quality approaches and management systems improve performance and meet the needs of the organisation.

Summary of learning outcomes

On completion of this module students will be able to:

- Describe and explain the scope of the global hospitality industry
- Understand the issues and influences affecting the hospitality industry
- Examine the role of branding within the hospitality sector
- Analyse the distinctive features of the accommodation and food service operations
- Investigate the importance of quality management

Syllabus		Chapter
Introduction to the global hospitality industry	Defining the global hospitality industry. The size and scope of the industry. Commercial and catering services sectors.	1
Social and economic issues and influences affecting the industry	Economic growth and decline, government stability, disposable income, socio-economic grouping, cultural influences. Internal and external influences. The industry's contribution to the economy.	2
The development of hotels and the hospitality industry	How the industry has changed in recent years, changes in fashion, technology, travel and business. Organisation and consumer trends in eating and drinking. Events that have shaped the industry.	3
The growth of global hospitality brands	Development of global hospitality brands. Branding strategies. Branding in international marketing.	4

Syllabus		Chapter
The accommodation industry: ▪ Business and conference hotels ▪ Resort hotels ▪ Budget hotels ▪ Boutique hotels ▪ Hostels and halls of residence	The size, nature and USP's of these sectors. The market, customers and locations. The product and service offering. Organisation and staffing. The operation of each type of accommodation. Current issues and future trends.	5
The foodservice industry: ▪ Restaurants ▪ Fast food outlets ▪ Contract catering, employee feeding ▪ Welfare catering ▪ Travel catering ▪ The licensed trade	Identifying the variety of establishments in the sector, different management structures, types of service offered and targeted customer base. Understanding typical operational styles of this sector, sector issues, operational issues and legal and statutory requirements. Identifying the trends in the food service industry. Operational systems and distribution systems. Legislation, current issues and future trends. Managing procedures specific to licensed retailing including generic and specific operating constraints, legal and statutory requirements.	6
Effective quality management in the global hospitality industry	Defining quality, the quality attributes and variables. Measuring and analysing quality standards. Improvement solutions to address the causes of defects and low quality products and service. Managing quality, TQM, costs and long-term benefits.	7

Assessment

This module will be assessed via a 2 ½ hour examination, set and marked by CTH. The examination will cover the whole of the assessment criteria in this unit and will take the form of 10 × 2 mark questions and 5 × 4 mark questions in section A (40 marks). Section B will comprise of 5 × 20 mark questions of which candidates must select and answer three (60 marks). CTH is a UK based awarding body and the syllabus content will in general reflect this. Any legislation and codes of practice will reflect the international nature of the industry and will not be country specific. International centres may find it advantageous to add local legislation or practice to their teaching but they should be aware that the CTH examination will not assess this local knowledge.

Further guidance

Recommended contact hours: 45
Credits: 10

Delivery strategies

It is strongly recommended that students are given the opportunity to visit a wide range of organisations to demonstrate the diverse nature of the industry. A programme of guest speakers will provide the student with a comprehensive understanding of the complexity of the global hospitality industry.

Recommended prior learning

There is no required prior learning however students must have completed formal education to 18 years old or equivalent and an interest in the hospitality industry is essential.

Resources

Learners need access to library and research facilities which should include some or all of the following:

Texts

- Brotherton, B *et al*,. (2003), *The International Hospitality Industry: Structure, Characteristics and Issues*, Butterworth Heinemann, ISBN 0750652950.
- Jones, P (2002), *An Introduction to Hospitality*, 2nd Edition, Thomson, ISBN 08264 6077-1.
- Kinton, R; Cesarani, V and Foskett, D (2007), *The Theory of Catering*, 11th Edition, Hodder and Stoughton, ISBN 0340939265.

Magazines and Journals

- The Caterer and Hotelkeeper (Reed Business Information)
- Chef (Reed Business Information)
- Croner's Catering Magazine (Croner Publications)
- Hospitality (Reed Business Information)
- Voice of the BHA (British Hospitality Industry)

Websites

www.bha-online.co.uk	British Hospitality Association
www.caterer.com	Caterer and Hotelkeeper
www.cateringnet.co.uk	The Catering Net
www.instituteofhospitality.org	The Institute of Hospitality
www.hospitalitynet.org	Hospitality Net
www.htf.org.uk	Hospitality Training Foundation
www.defra.gov.uk	Department for environment, food and rural affairs
www.biiab.org	British Institute of Innkeepers

Notes on the recommended texts

The module can be taught with the texts we have identified as relevant to the module syllabus. In keeping with a specialised qualification at this level there is no one text which covers the whole syllabus, but a number of texts which provide sufficient depth to explore the subject area. In general, the lecturer's lesson plans should be based on the module syllabus and supported by relevant texts, supplementary material familiar to the lecturer and the lecturer's experience. It is not essential to use all the recommended texts and lecturers should use their experience to decide which ones are most appropriate for their students. Where available and appropriate, past module examinations are also available to support lecturers.

CTH will always answer any questions from the centre's Head of Department either by e-mail or by phone.

The exam paper

All the CTH examinations for the Diploma in Hotel Management and Diploma in Tourism Management follow the same format.

Exam duration: 2½ hours

Section A

		Marks
Ten	2 mark questions	20
Five	4 mark questions	20
		40

All questions in Section A are compulsory

Section B

Five	20 mark questions (candidates must choose three)	60
		100

Other titles in this series

BPP Learning Media publishes the following titles for the CTH Diploma in Hotel Management:

- Food and Beverage Operations
- Food Hygiene, Health and Safety
- Front Office Operations
- Housekeeping and Accommodation Operations
- Finance for Tourism and Hospitality*
- Introduction to Business Operations*
- Marketing*
- The Tourism Industry*
- The Global Hospitality Industry

*These titles are also papers within the CTH Diploma in Tourism Management qualification.

In July 2010 BPP Learning Media will publish the remaining titles for the Diploma in Tourism Management:

- Travel Geography
- Travel Agency and Tour Guide Operations
- Introduction to Tourism Economics
- Special Interest Tourism
- Destination Analysis

CHAPTER 1

INTRODUCTION TO THE GLOBAL HOSPITALITY INDUSTRY

Chapter objectives

In this chapter you will:

- Be introduced to the 'global hospitality industry'
- Define the hospitality industry
- Investigate the growth of the hospitality industry
- Identify the size and scope of the industry
- Classify the catering and commercial service sectors

Topic list

Introduction to the global hospitality industry
History of the hospitality industry
Size and scope of the hospitality industry
Grading organisations
Other hospitality-related services

1 Introduction to the global hospitality industry

The tourism and hospitality industries are one of the world's largest sectors, amounting to '*over 10% of Gross Domestic Product* (GDP)' (*Cooper et al.*, 2005:4), and employing huge numbers of people; '*tourism employs 8% of the global workforce*' (www.tourismconcern.org.uk).

The hospitality industry, with its roots in the centuries old tradition of inn-keeping (*Jones*, 1996), has experienced huge growth in recent years: it recorded between 1990 and 1998 '*a growth of over 25% in the number of units*' (*Brotherton*, 2003:9) and a total of '*29.4 million bed spaces in hotels and similar establishments worldwide in 1997* (WTO, 2000). In the UK, the hospitality industry employs '*1.7 million people (6% of the working population)*' with the industry valued in the region of '*£55–60 billion a year*'. (www.caterersearch.com).

Expenditure (£bn), 2004 – 2006

	2004	*2005*	*2006*
Overnight accommodation	9.9	10.5	11.0
Eating out of home	19.0	19.6	20.7
Drinking out of home	34.7	34.9	35.6

Source: ONS Statistics

FOR DISCUSSION

Can you think of any hotels in your local area?

Are there any new hotels?

What type of hotels are they?

Are there any global branded or locally-owned hotels in your local area?

1.1 Defining hospitality

Due to its complex nature defining the 'hospitality industry' is very difficult. The Standard Industrial Classification (SIC) (1968) defined it as '*establishments (whether or not licensed for the sale of intoxicating liquors) providing meals, light refreshments, drink or accommodation*' (*Jones*, 1996). *Knowles* (1996:2) further describes the hospitality industry as *'any combination of the three core services of food, drink and accommodation...a blend of 'tangible and intangible elements' – and the service, atmosphere and image that surrounds them.*'

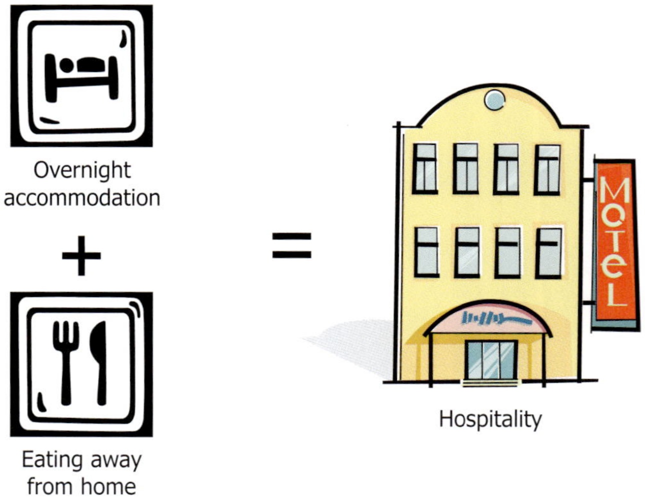

Jones (1996)

Figure 1.1: Defining hospitality

2 History of the hospitality industry

Antiquity to Middle Ages

- Thermal baths in villages for rest developed by the Greeks.
- Mansions to provide accommodation for travellers on government business built by the Romans.
- On Middle Eastern routes '*caravanserais*' established as a resting place for caravans.
- Monasteries and abbeys offered refuge to travellers.
- Religious orders built inns (but they did not yet offer meals), hospices and hospitals for those travelling.
- Numerous refuges for pilgrims and crusaders on their way to the Holy Land.
- Inns appeared in most of Europe, eg L'Auberge des Trois Rois in Basle.
- About the year 1200, staging posts for travellers and stations for couriers were set up in China and Mongolia.

16th-17th centuries

'The start of the hotel industry'

- At the beginning of the 15th century, the law in France required that hotels keep a register.
- English law also introduced rules for inns at a similar time.
- During the 16th century, more than 600 inns were registered in England.
- The first guide books for travellers were published in France.
- Signs were displayed outside establishments renowned for their refined cuisine.
- At the end of the 1600s, the first stage coaches to follow a regular timetable started operating in England.

18th-19th centuries

- The industrial revolution, (1760s), triggered the construction of hotels in mainland Europe, England and America.
- In New York and Copenhagen, hotels were established in city centres.
- Early 1800s, the Royal Hotel was built in London and holiday resorts constructed along the French and Italian rivieras.
- In Japan, Ryokan guest houses were established and in India, government-run Dak bungalows provided accommodation for travellers.
- The Tremont House in Boston was the first deluxe hotel in a city centre with inside toilets, locks on the doors and an *à la carte* menu.
- The Holt Hotel in New York City was the first to provide its guests with a lift for their luggage.
- Highway inns for stage coaches started to decline as trains began to replace horse-drawn transport.
- In New York, the New York Hotel was the first to be equipped with private bathrooms.
- In 1890 Le Grand Hôtel, Paris was the first entire hotel to be equipped with electric light.
- The Fifth Avenue Hotel in New York City was the first in that period to provide lifts for its guests.
- In 1880, the Sagamore Hotel in New York was the very first to provide electricity in all its rooms.
- In 1890 the first school for hoteliers was founded in Lausanne, Switzerland.

20th century

- In 1919 the Barcelona Ritz had bathrooms with hot and cold water!
- The Ritz and Savoy in London, le Négresco in Nice, the Plaza in New York, the Taj Mahal in Bombay were all constructed during this period.
- 1950s saw Club Méditerranée (G Trigano) develop the club village.
- In the 1960s new tourist resorts grew up around the Mediterranean: Spain, Greece, Yugoslavia thrived with the development of city and beach hotels.

Hotels for business people

- The 1970s witnessed the construction of hotels for business people.
- 'Black gold' (oil), attracted business people worldwide to the Middle-East.

The third hotel industry boom (1980s)

- Rise of hotels near airports, hotels for conferences, health hotels, ski holiday hotels, holiday villages and marina hotels.
- The first Property Management Systems (Fidelio, Hogatex, etc) appeared in the hospitality market.
- The Far East began developing hotels for business people and tourists began to discover China, South Korea, Thailand and Japan. American International chains prepared expansion plans to reach into Europe and the Middle- and Far East.

The 1990s: technology starts to make an impact

- Environment and energy conservation become important in marketing big chains.
- Reservation systems become more sophisticated enabling hotels to foster customer loyalty through database systems recording guest's individual history and individualised marketing programmes, satisfying guests' personal needs better than the competition.

(http://www.hospitalitynet.org/news/)

FOR DISCUSSION

What is the oldest hotel in your area / city? Why do you think this hotel was built?

Is the hotel still popular today? What types of tourists stay at the hotel?

3 Size and scope of the hospitality industry

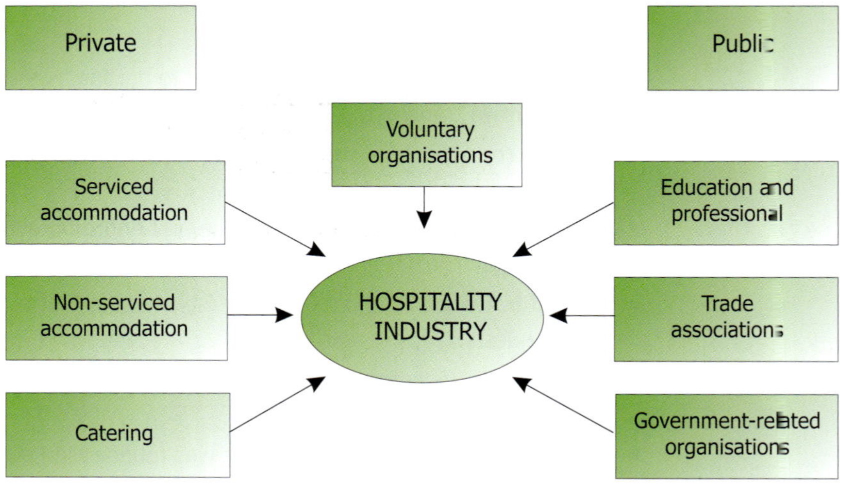

Figure 1.2: The hospitality sector

The hospitality sector includes '*all businesses that provide food, beverages, and/or accommodation services. This includes: restaurants; pubs, bars and clubs; hotels; contract catering; hospitality services.*' (www.prospects.ac.uk)

In the United Kingdom (UK) the hospitality industry is divided using the 'Standard Industrial Classification' (SIC), classifying the industry under 'Division 6' of the services industry and designated as 'Class 66' – '*Hotels & Catering*', which is then divided into six sub-groups.

Division 6		**Services**	
Class 66	**Group**	**Activity**	
			Hotels and Catering
	661		Restaurants, snack bars, cafes and other eating places
		6611	Eating places supplying food for consumption on the premises: (a) licensed (b) unlicensed
		6612	Take-away food shops
	662	6620	Public houses and bars
	663	6630	Nightclubs and licensed clubs
	664	6640	Canteens and messes (a) catering contractors (b) other canteens
	665	6650	Hotel trade (a) licensed (b) unlicensed
	667	6670	Other tourist or short-stay accommodation (a) camping and caravan sites (b) holiday camps (c) other tourist or short-stay accommodation

Source: Jones (2002)

Figure 1.3: Standard industrial classification of the hospitality industry

3.1 Private sector

3.1.1 Serviced and non-serviced accommodation

Generally, accommodation falls into two types: *'serviced and non-serviced'* as illustrated in the following table.

Accommodation types	
Serviced	**Non-serviced**
Hotels Formal accommodation offering full services. These can include: 'Country House Hotels' with big gardens set in the countryside or 'Metro Hotels' found in a city centre.	**Apartments, villas, cottages** Privately-owned by individuals or companies, where guests provide their own food and do their own cooking.
Guest houses Accommodation for more than six paying guests, with the owner and staff providing further services, for example, dinner.	**Campus accommodation** University halls of residences, where tourists can rent rooms, out of term time.

Accommodation types	
Serviced	**Non-serviced**
Bed & breakfast (B&B) Accommodation provided in a private house by the owner for up to six paying guests.	**Youth hostel** Generally basic accommodation, where guests stay in dormitories or rooms with other people and kitchen facilities are provided.
Farmhouses B&B or guest house accommodation provided on a working farm.	**Camp sites** Privately-owned land, where tourists pay a nightly-fee to pitch their tent or caravan, with washing and electricity sometimes provided.
Other accommodation: Time-share – tourists pay for access to an apartment for a set date over a number of years.	

3.1.2 The foodservice sector

This particular sector, also known as 'non-accommodation hospitality services', generally consists of: restaurants, fast-food outlets, cafeterias, public houses (pubs), bars, clubs and canteens.

(*Page & Connell*, 2006)

Sector	SIC classification	Differentiating factor
Restaurants	6111	'quintessential food service outlet'
Hotel foodservice	6650	'for people staying away from home'
Motorway & roadside	6611	'foodservice for the motorist'
Licensed trade	6620 and 6630	'food for people out for a drink'
Fast food and takeaways	6612 and 6611	'meal package for people in a hurry'
Employee-feeding	6640	'for people at their workplace'
Welfare catering	9310, 9320 and 9330	'for people unable to feed themselves'
Travel catering	–	'for people on the move'
Outside and social catering	–	'service where it was never intended'

Source: Jones (1997:117)

3.2 Government related hospitality organisations

3.2.1 Education and professional qualifications

Due to the growth of the service industries in recent years, training and education in the hospitality and catering industries has become paramount and many educational establishments and training organisations have sprung up to support existing and future employees within the industry to gain the necessary training and professional development they need.

Organisation	
Institute of Hospitality	*'To set and maintain standards of management, education, experience and practice for the benefits of its members, the industry and the general public.'* ▪ Provides qualifications for the hospitality industry. ▪ Sets industry standards. Website: http://www.instituteofhospitality.org/ (Formerly the HCIMA)
VT Training	▪ Advises and assists in the training of hotel and catering industry staff. ▪ Policies include: management development and training and training the unemployed. Website: http://www.vttraining.co.uk/vtt/courses-hospitality (Formerly HCTC)
Colleges and universities	Many educational establishments, including colleges and universities, have established qualifications in the hotel and catering sector at undergraduate and post-graduate level.

Trade Associations

Organisation	
British Hospitality Association (BHA)	▪ The industry's trade association provides a link between the industry and the 'public' sector: government, civil servants and other 'public sector' organisations. ▪ Represents companies such as the HCIMA. ▪ Publishes material for its members in relation to industry news. Website: http://www.bha.org.uk/

FOR DISCUSSION

Is there a similar organisation in your own country?

What is the purpose of the organisation?

4 Grading organisations

Most countries have a grading system for offered accommodation, and this generally follows a 5-star grading scheme, with one being the lowest and five being the highest. In the United Kingdom (UK) a number of organisations provide rating systems for the hospitality industry. This includes:

- AA – Automobile Association
- VisitBritain – National and regional tourist boards
- Michelin – including the 'world-renowned' restaurant and chef grading
- RAC – Royal Automobile Club

Gee (1994) explains that hotel grading systems are designed to fulfil a number of different needs. Five of the most important are:

- **Standardisation**: to establish a system of uniform service and product quality that helps to create an orderly travel market distribution system for buyers and sellers.
- **Marketing**: to advertise travellers on the range and type of hotels available within a destination as a means of promoting the destination and encouraging healthy competition in the market-place

- **Consumer protection**: to ensure that the hotel meets minimum standards of accommodation, facilities, and service within classification and grade definitions.
- **Revenue generation**: to provide revenue from licensing, the sale of guidebooks, and so forth.
- **Control**: to provide a system for controlling general industry quality.

The following table details the hotel grading system in the UK, based on the AA (Automobile Association) accommodation grading standards.

Star rating	Hotel
★	Courteous staff provide an informal yet competent service. The majority of rooms are en suite, and a designated dining area serves breakfast daily and dinner most evenings.
★★	All rooms are en suite or have private facilities. A restaurant or dining room serves breakfast daily and dinner most evenings.
★★★	Staff are smartly and professionally presented. All rooms are en suite, and the restaurant or dining room is open to residents and non-residents.
★★★★	Professional, uniformed staff respond to your needs or requests, and there usually are well-appointed public areas. The restaurant or dining room is open to residents and non-residents, and lunch is available in a designated eating area.
★★★★★	Luxurious accommodation and public areas, with a range of extra facilities and a multilingual service available. Guests are greeted at the hotel entrance. High quality menu and wine list.

FOR DISCUSSION

Do the grading systems operate on a similar system in your own country?

Do you think all destinations have all of these grading ranges from 1 star to 5 stars?

Number of hotels inspected by the AA, 2006

	1*	2*	3*	4*	5*	Budget
UK	14	638	1,623	665	8	621

4.1 The AA Rosette System

Rosette awards for hotels with restaurants

Rosettes are awarded annually to AA inspected restaurants for the quality of their food. Most star-rated hotels have their own restaurants which are regularly inspected. Not all restaurants receive an AA award, but will generally serve enjoyable food of a reasonable standard.

(1 rosette)	Excellent restaurants that stand out in their local area. The food is prepared with care, understanding and skill, using good-quality ingredients.
(2 rosettes)	The best local restaurants, offering higher standards and better consistency. Greater precision is apparent in the cooking, and there is obvious attention to the quality and selection of ingredients.

	Three Rosettes are awarded to outstanding restaurants that demand recognition well beyond the local area. The highest quality ingredients receive sympathetic treatment, and there is consistent timing, seasoning, and judgement of flavour combinations You can expect excellent and intelligent service, and a well-chosen wine list.
	Four Rosettes highlight cooking that demands national recognition. Dishes demonstrate intense ambition, a passion for excellence, superb technical skills and remarkable consistency. An appreciation of culinary traditions is combined with a desire for exploration and improvement.
	The food at a Five Rosette restaurant stands comparison with the best in the world. It is highly individual, benefits from breathtaking culinary skills, and sets the standards to which others aspire. There will also be a knowledgeable and distinctive wine list.

Source: The AA (2009)

Advantages and disadvantages of grading systems

Advantages	Disadvantages
▪ Maintains standards within sector ▪ Assists with marketing of establishments ▪ Assists customers in selecting hotels	▪ Not all accommodation is graded (not compulsory) ▪ A quality system does not always guarantee quality ▪ Grading can vary from one country to another (for example, a 4-star hotel in China may be a different standard to a four star hotel in the US). This disparity can affect customer satisfaction.

ACTIVITY 1 **2 minutes**

Can a hospitality operation have only one membership with one grading system?

The Burj Al Arab Hotel, Dubai, United Arab Emirates, the most luxurious hotel in the world.

Source: http://thebuilderblog.files.wordpress.com/2008/03/_editor_burj_al_arab_01.jpg

FOR DISCUSSION

The Burj Al Arab Hotel claims to be of 7-star standard and the most luxurious hotel in the world. Visit the website below and discuss how it achieves its 7-star standard?

Website: https://www.jumeirah.com/en/Hotels-and-Resorts/Destinations/Dubai/Burj-Al-Arab/

(Feedback to this discussion activity is given at the end of the chapter)

Gee (1994) explains some guidelines for attaining World-Class Status.

'There must be a shared vision within the organisation of what constitutes a great hotel.

Management must not always be by the book. Managers must do more than routine things, and they must do much more than simply what is necessary.

Managers must know how to play host to people from all walks and stations of life, coming from any part of the world.

The hotel must be valued by its host community and should be an involved contributor to the community's social aspirations and goals.

Culture must be understood, respected, and adopted as a resource in the hotel's internal value system.

Human resources must be treated as investment assets. Policies, procedures, rules, and practices must all reflect this philosophy.

Training must be continuous at all levels. Perfection is a journey, not a destination.

Communication must not be happenstance. It is an integral part of the organisation and employees must have systematic access to information.

The marketplace is the final judge of what is world-class. The delivery system must fulfill the promise made through marketing. The customer's trust and the hotel's credibility are two sides of the same coin.

Details matter. The hotel business is a business of details, attitudes, promises, and expectations. It is not a manufacturing environment – the rules of heavy industry have no application except for quality control principles applied at the customer service level.

Perception is reality in the external world. Management must therefore have ways of measuring or assessing the image of the hotel in order to find ways for its continuous improvement. It is always harder to achieve and maintain a reputation than to lose it.'

5 Other hospitality-related services

Accommodation and food are often only part of the product with other hospitality-related services a key way for a hotel to differentiate from its competitors.

Activity	
Gambling	Casino divisions within hotel and catering companies. Examples: Rank Organisation, Stakis and Stanley Leisure
Sport	▪ **Active**: many hotels have health centres and gyms for guests and for private members ▪ **Passive**: some hotels put on sports events so as to bring in sports fans to watch major events such as boxing, for example the MGM Grand, Las Vegas
Visitor attractions	Some visitor attractions, in particular the larger, purpose-built resorts include many hotels and catering facilities as a part of their product. Examples include the Disney Resorts, and major theme parks including Alton Towers, UK.

CHAPTER SUMMARY

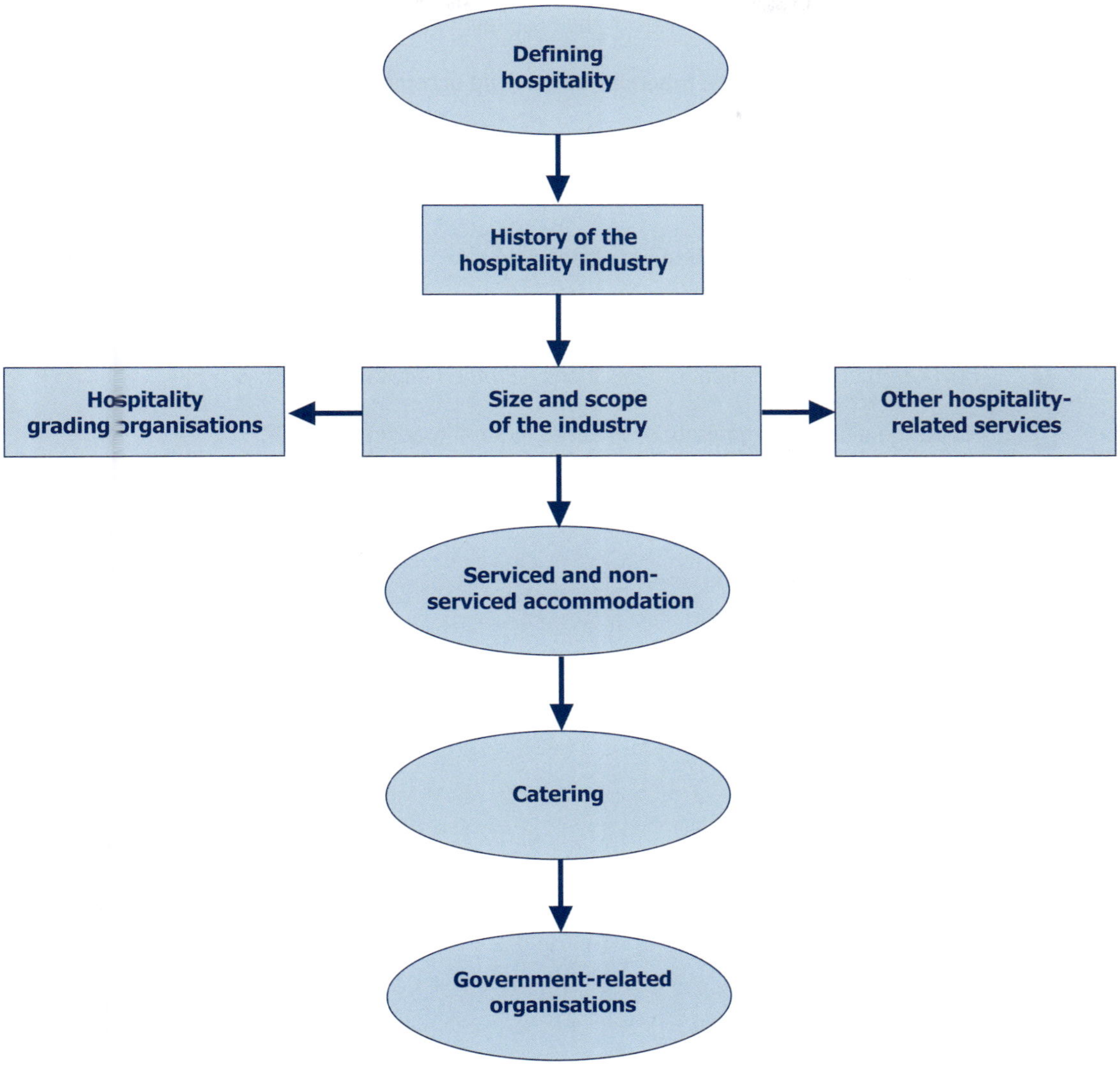

SELF-TEST QUESTIONS

1. What are the three core services of the hospitality industry?
2. Name a minimum of three examples of 'serviced accommodation.'
3. Name a minimum of three types of 'non-serviced' accommodation.
4. Describe three 'foodservice sectors'.
5. What is the role of the Institute of Hospitality?
6. Identify the different levels of government involvement in tourism.
7. How can these government organisations help the hospitality industry?
8. Name the different organisations involved in hotel grading in the UK.
9. Name some other hospitality-related activities with appropriate examples.

SELF-TEST ANSWERS

1. According to *Knowles* (1996:2) the three core services of the hospitality industry are: 'food, drink and accommodation'.

2. Examples of serviced accommodation include: hotels, guest houses, bed & breakfasts and farmhouses.

3. Examples of 'non-serviced' accommodation can include: apartments, villas, gites, cottages, campus accommodation, youth hostels and campsites.

4. Any three from the table 'The catering sector' in Section 1.3.2.

5. The Institute of Hospitality is a regulatory body who: '*sets and maintains standards of management, education, experience and practice for the benefits of its members, the industry and the general public*', by providing qualifications for the hospitality industry and industry standards within a 'Code of Conduct'.

6. National Tourist Boards (NTB), Regional Tourist Boards (RTB) and Local Authorities (LA).

7. National Tourist Boards help to encourage domestic tourism through marketing activities' active promotion of the destination in a variety of media, travel exhibitions and conferences, one of the largest being the World Travel Markets (WTM). They also encourage the development of attractions and facilities by allowing permission for construction of buildings and infrastructure. NTBs also advise central government on tourism matters, from data they have acquired through market research and statistics.

   Regional Tourist Boards also encourage regional tourism, through marketing activities and encourage the development of amenities and facilities (infrastructure and superstructure).

   Local Authorities act for smaller regions within a Regional Tourist Board. They are concerned with the provision of facilities in the local area, by authorising and planning schemes relating to infrastructure and superstructure. They may also control land use. Furthermore, LAs provide signage directing people to tourist attractions and run Tourist Information Centres (TIC).

8. The different organisations involved in hotel grading in the UK include:

   - AA – Automobile Association
   - VisitBritain
   - Michelin – including the 'world-renowned' restaurant and chef grading
   - The RAC – Royal Automobile Club

9. Other hospitality-related activities include:

   - **Gambling** – The Rank Organisation
   - **Active sports** – health centres and gyms for guests and for private members
   - **Passive sports-related activities** – major sports events, such as boxing at the MGM Grand, Las Vegas, to attract a large number of sports fans.

ANSWER TO ACTIVITY

1. No, hospitality operations can be members of more than one hotel grading system.

FEEDBACK TO DISCUSSION QUESTION

The Burj Al Arab Hotel claims to be of 7-star standard and the most luxurious hotel in the world.

Your answer could include: high staff to customer ratios, superior design, accommodation is entirely made up of suites, extensive in-room facilities, highly skilled employees, advanced technology throughout used to achieve customer satisfaction, butler service for each suite, food and beverage facilities offering world class cuisine. You may have thought of other services equally important to the hotel's rating.

CHAPTER 2

SOCIAL AND ECONOMIC ISSUES AND INFLUENCES AFFECTING THE INDUSTRY

Chapter objectives

In this chapter you will:

- Be introduced to external factors affecting the industry
- Investigate the socio-cultural influences on the industry
- Identify the socio-cultural impacts
- Interpret the economic influences
- Determine the economic impacts of the industry

Topic list

1 Introduction to social and economic issues and influences

Tourism is a huge industry, *'probably the single most important industry in the world'* (*Holloway*, 2006:92) and due to its size and labour intensive nature, estimates range from '*127 million people* [employed] *around the world* (*Holloway*, 2006:92), to '*207 million jobs*' (*Page & Connell*, 2006:343). Developing countries in particular use tourism as a way of generating income, due to the abundance of benefits tourism can bring: '*the number of hotel units in Western Asia grew by 54.1%, and in the Eastern Asia and Pacific region the number grew by 45.4%, from 1990–1998*. (*Litteljohn*, 2003:11)

This chapter will look at the social and economic issues and influences affecting the industry.

1.1 Factors affecting the hospitality industry

PEST analysis can be performed to determine the factors that affect any type of industry. External PEST factors may have both positive and negative impacts for an organisation, but as these factors are outside its control the organisation can only react by planning a strategy which might turn potential threats into opportunity.

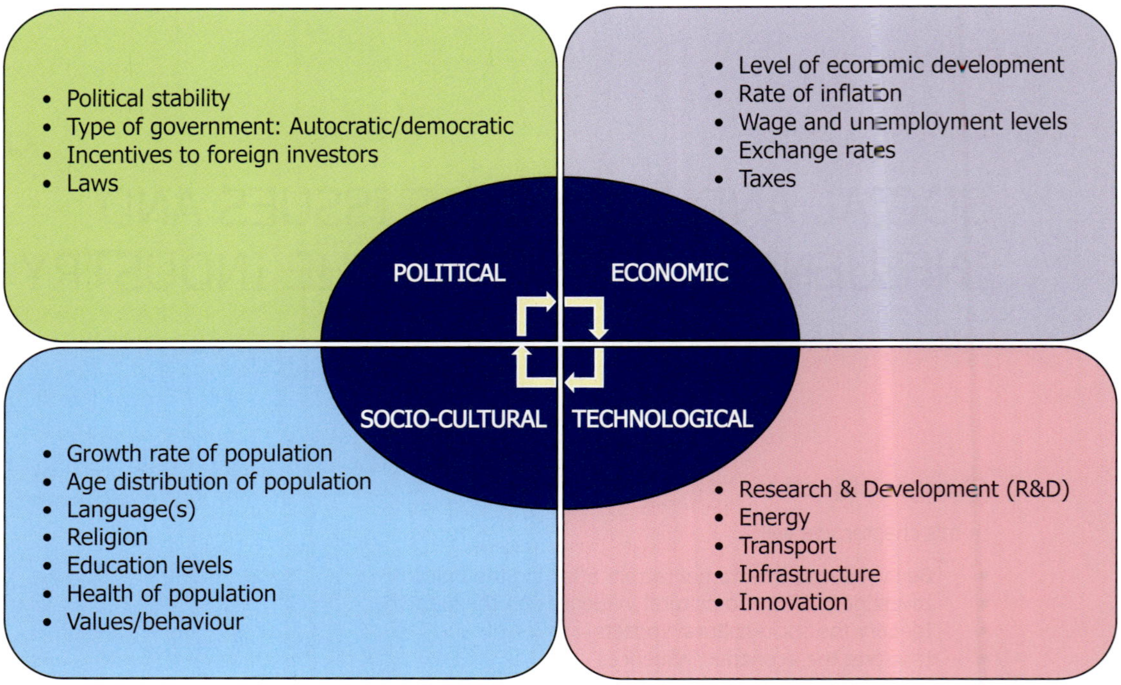

Figure 2.1: PEST analysis for an organisation

ACTIVITY 1 **30 minutes**

For an organisation of your choice, perform a PEST analysis.

Environmental issues have become a major factor in more recent times. What environmental issues can affect the hospitality industry?

1.2 Socio-cultural influences

Page & Connell (2006), identify two categories of socio-cultural influences:

- Personal and family influences
- Social and situational influences

1.2.1 Personal and family influences

Age	Age (demographic) can have a huge influence on the type of destination travelled to and the type of accommodation required. Younger adults may be attracted to more 'active holidays', or entertainment, therefore they would be attracted to accommodation that offers bars, restaurants, nightclubs, water-sports and excursions, or is conveniently located to nightlife and activities. Older tourists, on the other hand, may want holidays that involve more 'passive' pursuits or more safe and secure activities, and they may be attracted to quieter, more comfortable accommodation.
Family life cycle	The stage at which a family is at or the family life cycle is also an influencing factor. (See Figure 2.2). A family with young children will want to stay in accommodation with lots of activities for children or 'Kids' Clubs'. Teenagers may want 'clubs/bars', not necessarily appreciated by retirees.
Gender	**Women**: Voluntary work, or a break from caring (spa breaks) are popular among women (*Kinnaird & Hall*, 1994). Lone travel is perceived as brave, not normal, as women feel vulnerable (*Kinnaird & Hall*, 1994). Passive activities are preferred (*Foo et al.,* 2004). More women are now in the workplace. To capitalise on this trend hotels are having to meet their specific needs. Marriott in some properties feature a 'female floor' exclusively for female travellers. Rooms feature soft colour design, women's magazines and toiletries. All female floors appeal to the safety concerns of independent female travellers. **Men**: For men lone travel is more acceptable. Adventurous, more active pursuits are preferred, particularly 'adventure holidays' (*Foo et al.*, 2004).
Disability	Some barriers exist for less-abled persons: ▪ Internal: ineffective social skills, health, physical, psychological. ▪ Economic: need travel companions, special facilities. ▪ Environmental: architectural, accessibility, ecological – paths, hills, transport, rules & regulations, safety. ▪ Interactive: communication, attitudes of industry workers, information availability/accuracy.

Murray & Sproats (1990)

1.2.2 The family life cycle

Source: Epilepsyfoundation.org

Stage	Characteristics	Tourism/Hospitality behaviour
Early childhood	Entirely dependent on parent or guardian. Classic sun, sea and sand (3 Ss) holiday.	Seaside or inland resort, with entertainment for children.
Early teenager	More influence on decision-making, but still dependent on parents.	Resort-based holidays with nightlife. Group-based holidays.
Young person	Young, single, not living at home.	Sunlust – Wanderlust. Adventure, backpacking and experiences.
Partnership stage	Couples living together, 'young professionals'. Time constraints on travel.	All types of holidays, many short breaks ('city breaks'), to fit-in with careers. Example: Sandals Resorts
Family stage – early	Families, single parents, separated with young children.	Main holidays (mass tourism) and Visiting Friends and Relatives (VFR). Companies that would target this market include Disney, Warner Holidays, Butlins, Centreparcs, and all-inclusive resorts
Family stage – late	With children at secondary school, only take holidays outside term-time.	Mix of holidays, children wanting a level of independence – activities, clubs.
Empty nest	Children leave home, parents more freedom and disposable income.	More expensive holidays: long-haul, cruises, and second breaks. Examples: Saga Holidays, P&O Cruises
Retired	One person or partners retired, income fixed, lots of free-time.	More passive, better quality holidays.

Source: Amended from Lumsdon (1997:44)

Figure 2.2: The family life cycle (North American/European Model)

ACTIVITY 2 **20 minutes**

For each of the different stages, listed opposite, think of an appropriate type of accommodation, justifying why this is suitable.

1.2.3 Social and situational issues

Nationality and national identity	This can include: **Language barriers** – which may discourage some people to travel abroad. **Legal requirements** – visa acquisition difficulties may prevent or deter travel for some nationalities.
Tourism and work	**Time** – the more people work, the less time they have to travel and *vice-versa*. **Nature of work** – if people's work is boring, they use travel as means to 'escape'.
Social class and income	Society may be divided into groups (**socio-economic grouping**), classified by certain jobs, level of further education, and social characteristics. The higher status groups tend to travel more, take overseas holidays, travel more independently and take more frequent 'short-break' holidays.

Social grade	Social status	Occupation
A	Upper middle class	Higher managerial, professional
B	Middle class	Intermediate managerial, professional
C1	Lower middle class	Supervisory, junior management
C2	Skilled working class	Skilled manual workers
D	Working class	Semi/unskilled
E	Lowest level	Pensioners, casual, unemployed

Figure 2.3: Socio-economic groups

FOR DISCUSSION

Using the socio-economic grouping table think of different types of holidays suitable for each group. In respect of these types of holidays what do you think would be the accommodation requirements?

2 Socio-cultural impacts of tourism and hospitality

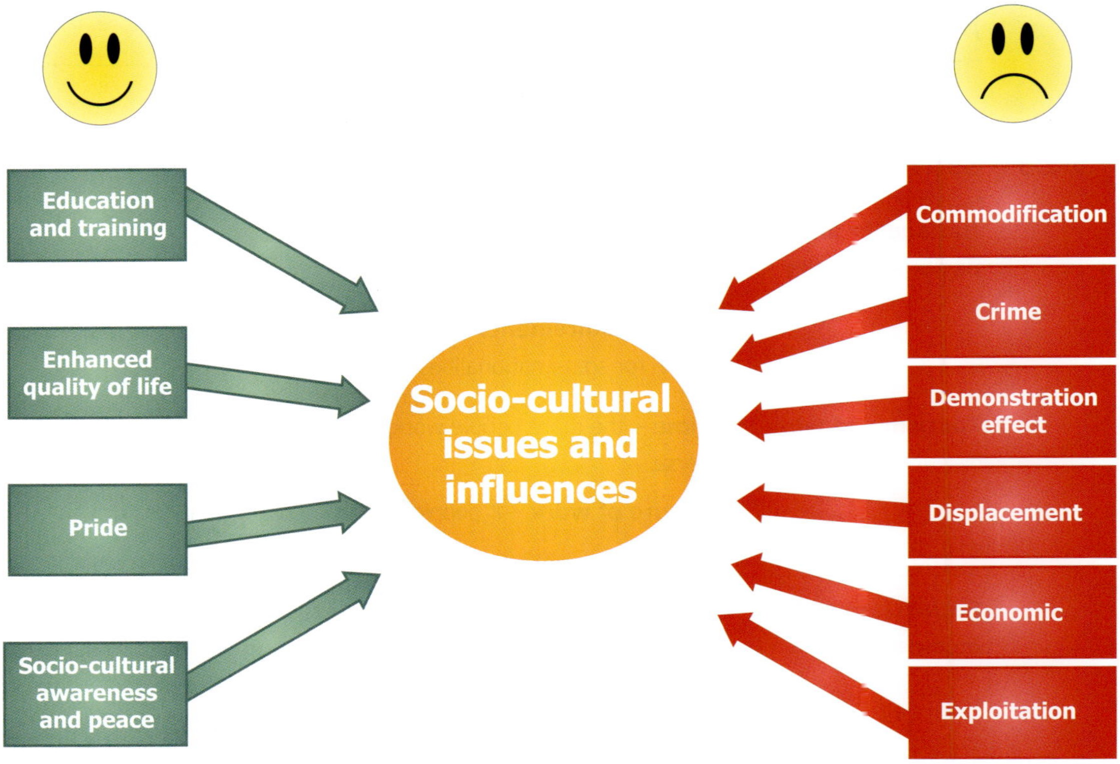

2.1 Positive socio-cultural impacts of hospitality and tourism

Positive socio-cultural impacts of hospitality and tourism	
Education and training	Hospitality and tourism can provide the opportunity for locals to learn new skills and qualifications, which are essential for their work in the industry. This may include the major hotel organisations training and educating staff in the areas of customer service and IT, essential for dealing with international customers and reservations and ticketing.
Enhanced quality of life	Investment can help to improve the local infrastructure and superstructure: roads, sanitation, shops and facilities, which can all be used by locals. Furthermore, increasing incomes from locally-owned businesses and more local jobs means that the 'host' population may have more money to spend (disposable income).
Pride	With an increase in visitors and investment comes an increase in 'local pride'. Tourists want to 'experience' the local culture of the destination and witness local ceremonies, rituals, skills and crafts. This can give the 'host' population a renewed interest in their own heritage and make them feel proud of their own culture.
Socio-cultural awareness and peace	Tourism and hospitality enables people from different cultures to meet and gain a greater knowledge through personal exchange and interaction. This 'first hand' cultural exchange can create a greater understanding between peoples, in terms of beliefs, customs, language and religion.

2.2 Negative socio-cultural impacts of tourism and hospitality

Negative socio-cultural impacts of hospitality and tourism	
Commodification	'Commodification' is where ceremonies, cultural performances and rituals '*are changed to suit the needs and wishes of tourists*' (*Cooper et al.*, 2005:242). These performances and ceremonies are made more colourful and dramatic so '*culture becomes a commodity for financial transactions*' (*Cooper et al.*, 2005:243), and does not really show the 'real' culture of the destination: also referred to as 'staged authenticity'.
Crime	Crime is common in many popular destinations. Tourists take substantial amounts of money and valuables such as digital cameras and mp3 players. The indigenous population may not be able to afford these items and see the tourists in an unfamiliar environment as an easy target. Furthermore, some visitors on holiday may want to have very different experiences than they would in their usual environments; and potentially illegal experiences such as taking drugs or prostitution ('sex tourism').
Demonstration effect	'*Changes in attitudes, values or behaviour which can result from merely observing tourists*' (*De Kadt*, 1979). The host population see the tourists' behaviour, clothes and possessions and try to emulate (copy) them. This can lead to a loss of identity of the local culture, in particular among the younger population, who turn to more 'western' styles of clothes and music: 'westernisation'.
Displacement	The potential economic benefits of tourism, leads to the development of tourism infrastructure and superstructure. These constructions often mean that large areas of land are needed, and this can often be land where the indigenous population live, 'local people being moved away from their place of residence to make way for tourism development have been recorded' (*Page & Connell*, 2006: 368).
Economic	Tourism can have a huge economic impact on a destination, and in turn on the local population. It can lead to increased prosperity of the local population, which can cause social tensions between incoming migrants looking for work, and the 'host' population. Furthermore, with the increasing popularity of a destination and the resources needed to support the industry, prices, for example of housing due to 'second home ownership' and taxes may increase, putting greater financial pressure on the local population, again causing resentment. In some situations large chains entering certain areas may have a severe negative impact on revenues of local businesses.
Exploitation	Tourism may create jobs but sometimes these jobs are not as 'attractive' as they may initially seem, when some organisations exploit the local population. Child labour, forced labour and lower level jobs for locals are some examples of how organisations, including some 'globalised' companies, are reaping the economic benefits of tourism for their own advantage.

3 Economic influences

Economic growth and a strong economy is extremely beneficial for tourism and consequently, for the hospitality industry. Conversely, slow economic growth (or negative growth – 'recession') can have a very negative impact. As *Dr Peter Tarlow* states '*the tourism industry is an integral component of the global economy and there is no doubt that tourism will be affected by the outbreak of global economic volatility*' (www.eturbonews.com). As *Bierman* (2008) states '*demand for luxury end of the market is likely to decrease while demand for either low cost or perceived good value products and services is likely to grow and there is likely to be a growth in domestic travel or short haul international travel as people choose to stay closer to home.*'

3.1 Factors influencing hospitality spending

Factor	
Discretionary expense	During tough economic times, people conserve their cash to cover the essentials of life: food, shelter and family necessities, therefore, this decreases the money people spend on non-essential items, such as travel and leisure.
Exchange rates	The rise and fall of currencies (fluctuations) can have a huge impact on tourism and hospitality industries, especially in terms of foreign travel. In particular, 2009 was regarded as the year of the 'staycation' in the UK, as many people decided to stay in the UK for their vacations, due to the weakness of pound sterling (£) against the euro (€).
Disposable income	The amount of income left to an individual after direct taxes (such as PAYE, income tax) have been deducted and essential expenses (such as food, clothing, shelter) have been paid is 'disposable income'. During difficult economic times, spending on non-essentials decreases, as people are concerned with reducing costs and increasing savings. Example: In 2009 a world-wide recession caused consumers to reduce their spending. In the UK one of the effects was for more consumers to use budget hotels and to eat more meals at home to reduce expenditure.

3.2 Economic impacts of tourism and hospitality

As stated, tourism is a huge industry, and with it, there are some very attractive economic benefits: '*in 2004, worldwide tourism receipts, excluding international fares, reached $622 billion*' (WTO). It accounts for '*11% of Gross Domestic Product*' (WTTC), therefore, many countries, in particular developing countries are constantly looking at tourism as a way to generate their economies. Further, it is becoming cheaper and easier for people to travel and the increasing wealth of some of the largest nations on earth, most notably China and India, is making tourism an even more attractive proposition for economic growth.

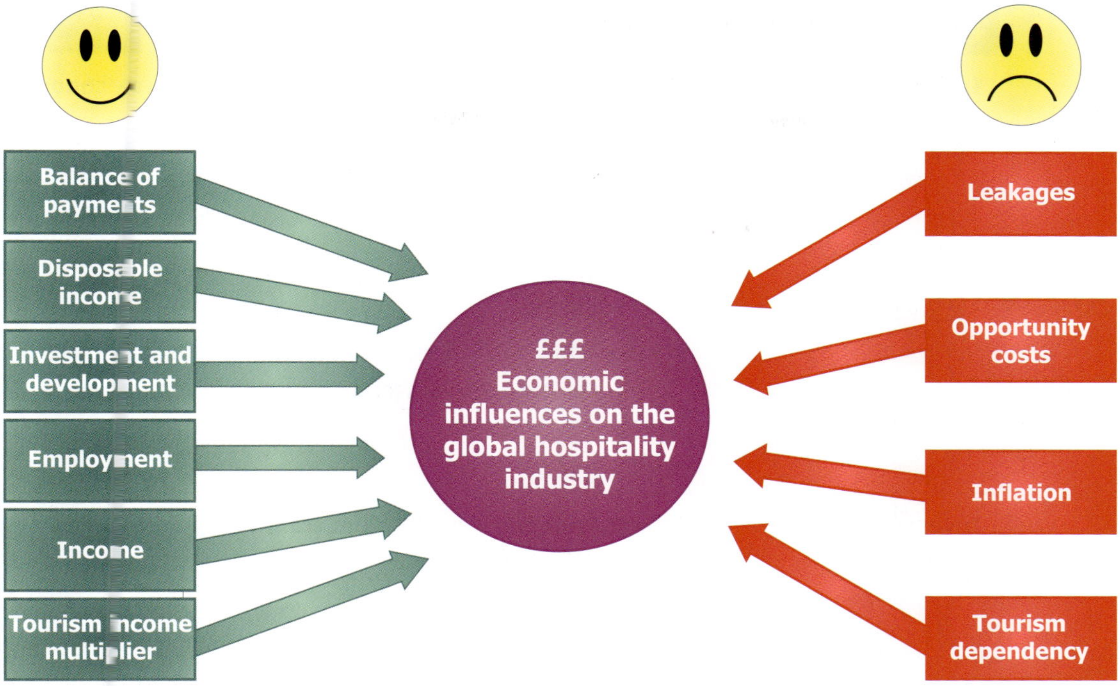

Figure 2.4: The positive and negative economic impacts of the global hospitality industry

3.2.1 The positive economic impacts of the industry

Positive economic issues	
Balance of payments	'*The quantity of a country's own currency flowing out of the country minus the amount flowing in*'. (http://economics.about.com) Hospitality and tourism are good industries to reduce or minimise a country's 'balance of payments'. Tourists bring the destination currency into the receiving country (exchanged in the overseas country), or they exchange their own currency in the destination. This means that the money spent by the tourist in the destination is 'credited' to the receiving country's economy, and 'debited' from the tourist's own country, meaning that the host country is receiving more money from outside its borders. This is extremely beneficial for countries receiving tourists from 'high value' currency countries, such as the European Union Zone, the United States and the United Kingdom.
Employment	▪ **Direct employment**: these are jobs directly involved in the industry, for example working in a hotel. ▪ **Indirect employment**: jobs created in the supply sector, for example a laundry company. ▪ **Induced employment**: these are jobs created due to increased wealth of the locals from tourism, and the locals spending more money in their local economy.

Positive economic issues	
Income	**Tourism creates money in a destination's local economy**, through: ▪ **Wages and salaries** – from the locals' employment in the local area (directly, indirectly or induced). ▪ **Profits** – with local businesses making money from the tourists. ▪ **Rent** – from leasing accommodation to tourists and 'migrating' workforce. ▪ **Tax** – the 'public purse' also benefits from tourist expenditure, in the form of taxes, either a local tax or a national tax, such as Value Added Tax (VAT), which can then go towards further investment in the local or national economy.
Investment and development	**Investment and development from the 'public' sector (government) or private sector**. ▪ **Public** – The government may want to develop the area, by investing in the infrastructure and superstructure of a destination, to make it more accessible and attractive for tourism. This may mean the construction of new roads, airports and telecommunications. ▪ **Private** – Many companies, in particular multinational companies (MNCs), may see the area as being an attractive place to set up some operations. This in turn can lead to further investment from other 'large' organisations investing in the area: 'Multiplier Effect'.
Multiplier effect	**Tourism can have many positive 'knock-on' effects**, **'the Multiplier Effect'**, **meaning that** '*tourist expenditure will inject additional cash flow into the regional economy and increase regional income*'. (*Page & Connell*, 2006:353) ▪ **Employment multiplier**: further jobs (indirect and induced) are created by direct tourism employment. ▪ **Income multiplier**: additional income is created in an economy as a result of direct tourist expenditure. The locals have more money from the employment multiplier, which they in turn, spend in the local economy in shops, supermarkets and so on.

'The money spent by tourists in the area will be re-spent by recipients (other businesses and locals) in the area'.
(*Holloway*, 2006:103).

3.2.2 The negative economic impacts of the industry

Negative economic impacts	
Dependency	Some countries are 'economically dependent' on tourism and hospitality, especially some less developed countries (LDC), which may have few other industries. Therefore, if tourism is lost or decreases in their country (credit crunch, natural disasters or political instability), they could lose a lot of income and this could have a huge impact on their national economies, in terms of loss of revenue, balance of payments and taxes.
Inflation	Generally with increased demand comes increased inflation, which means that the prices and values of land and products, increases. Locals may not be able to continue to afford to live and invest in businesses in the area, which in turn could lead to negative socio-cultural impacts of tourism.
Leakages	'*Money that drops out of circulation within a local economy, by being saved or spent on goods and services outside the economy*'. (*Cooper et al.*, 2005:794) Tourism and hospitality may attract a lot of investment, but in many cases the investment is from companies outside the borders of the receiving country, especially 'multinational companies' (MNCs). Many of these MNCs, have their headquarters (HQ) located in different countries, therefore the profit made from the tourist activity does not stay in the host destination, it goes back to the country of residence of the company's HQ. Leakage can also occur when a country or destination has to purchase items from outside the economy 'import' (national or local). This is a particular issue for small island states, which have to 'buy-in' goods to satisfy the tastes and needs of tourists from more larger, developed nations, especially 'Psycho-centric Tourists'.
Opportunity costs (displacement effect)	'*Developing tourism at the expense of other activities or areas of investment.*' (*Page & Connell*, 2006:350) This is money (public) that if invested in tourism, is not available for other uses. Local communities could lose out on facilities and infrastructure that they need. A 'cost-benefit analysis' can be performed to determine the best way to invest the money, but in many cases the local population's needs are neglected.

FOR DISCUSSION

Think about the tourist areas in your region.

Are the prices of goods more expensive in the tourist area compared to where you live?

Are there any big hotels and fast-food places in the tourist area? What are the names of these hotels and fast-food restaurants? Are any of the hotels and fast-food restaurants locally-owned?

CHAPTER SUMMARY

SELF-TEST QUESTIONS

1. What is PEST?
2. Identify the personal and family influences on the hospitality industry.
3. List the six different socio-economic groups.
4. Identify the positive and negative socio-cultural impacts.
5. What does TIM stand for?
6. Explain the TIM model.
7. Identify and explain the negative economic impacts on the industry.

SELF-TEST ANSWERS

1 PEST stands for: Political, Economic, Socio-cultural and Technological factors, that is uncontrollable external influences on an organisation.

2 Personal and family influences on the industry include: **Age**: the age of the tourist can influence the type of destination and accommodation required, eg people in their 20s may want a hotel with lots of entertainment, and located near 'nightlife'. **Family life cycle**: a family with young children will want to stay in accommodation with lots of activities for children or 'Kids' Clubs'. Gender: women may want accommodation that is safe and secure, and possibly relaxing. **Disability**: people with disabilities may require accommodation that is easily accessible or with facilities to help them with their needs.

3

Social grade	Social status	Occupation
A	Upper middle class	Higher managerial, professional
B	Middle class	Intermediate managerial, professional
C1	Lower middle class	Supervisory, junior management
C2	Skilled working class	Skilled manual workers
D	Working class	Semi/unskilled
E	Lowest level	Pensioners, casual, unemployed

4 The positive socio-cultural impacts can include: education and training, enhanced quality of life, pride, socio-cultural awareness and peace.

The negative socio-cultural impacts include: commodification, crime, demonstration effect, displacement and exploitation.

5 TIM stands for Tourism Income Multiplier and involves the money spent by tourists in the area will be re-spent by recipients (other businesses and locals) in the area.

6 As stated by *Holloway* (2006:103) the Tourism Income Multiplier (TIM) is *'the money spent by tourists in the area which will be re-spent by recipients (other businesses and locals) in the area'.*

The money tourists spend in the area is received (income) by local hotel and business owners, such as shops, bars and restaurants. Once this money is received by proprietors it is distributed into many different areas of the local economy, in the form of **taxes** (such as local council taxes), **spending** (the owners need to pay staff wages and salaries, which in turn is spent in the local economy by employees, ie rent or mortgages for accommodation, and in local shops and supermarkets). Furthermore, the owners of local businesses have to replace the goods they have sold therefore they need to purchase extra stock and items, purchased from local suppliers, such as wholesalers located in the local area.

On occasions, some of the money spent by tourists does not enter the local economy. Some of the tourist's income has to pay for national taxes, such as Value Added Taxes (VAT) and National Insurance Moreover, some of the income is retained and saved by the local business owners. Finally, due to the global nature of the industry, many tourism and hospitality organisations are '**multinational companies**' (MNC), and they have their headquarters located in countries outside of the borders where the money is received (**leakages**), therefore the profits go to the country where the multinational company is based, and 'leaks' from the economy where the money is received.

7 Negative economic impacts of tourism are: leakages; money lost from the local economy, opportunity costs; money which could be spent in other areas, such as education or health, inflation; the increasing prices of goods and services and tourism dependency; where the region is dependent on the industry and does not have any other industry to generate money, a risky situation.

ANSWERS TO ACTIVITIES

1 Environmental issues can include factors such as: pollution: aesthetic, noise, water and air.

2 **Stage**

- **Early childhood** – this would be for families with young children, therefore accommodation that provides a safe environment, away from busy roads, and facilities and entertainment, such as kids' clubs and child care facilities.
- **Early teenager** – again for families, the type of accommodation should provide 'family entertainment' such as clubs and activities, such as sports. The hotel should be a safe and secure environment, possibly with laid-on entertainment and excursions.
- **Young person** – this relates to persons in their late teens, or early twenties. This group would like to be in a location with nightlife, and the accommodation should provide social areas, such as bars and nightclubs.
- **Partnership stage** – people who are yet without children. This group would prefer accommodation with some nightlife and entertainment, and social areas such as bars and restaurants.
- **Family stage – early** – families with younger children, kids' clubs and a safe and secure environment are paramount.
- **Family stage – late** – families with teenagers, therefore entertainment activities for teenagers, and a safe and secure environment.
- **Empty nest** – children have left home, therefore this is mainly more mature couples. This group will want social areas, such as bars and restaurants, but also a location that is not too noisy.
- **Retired** – this group may be persons as couples or singles. Older people, they will probably require some form of less active (passive) activities, and in a quiet location.

CHAPTER 3

THE DEVELOPMENT OF HOTELS AND THE HOSPITALITY INDUSTRY

Chapter objectives

In this chapter you will:

- Be introduced to the growth of the tourism and hospitality industry
- Determine the factors influencing the development of the industry

Topic list

1 The increase in international tourism

'*In 2004, worldwide tourism receipts, excluding international fares, reached $622 billion*' (WTO).

The global significance of tourism has developed as more people are travelling than ever before and forecasts indicate that this number will continue to rise.

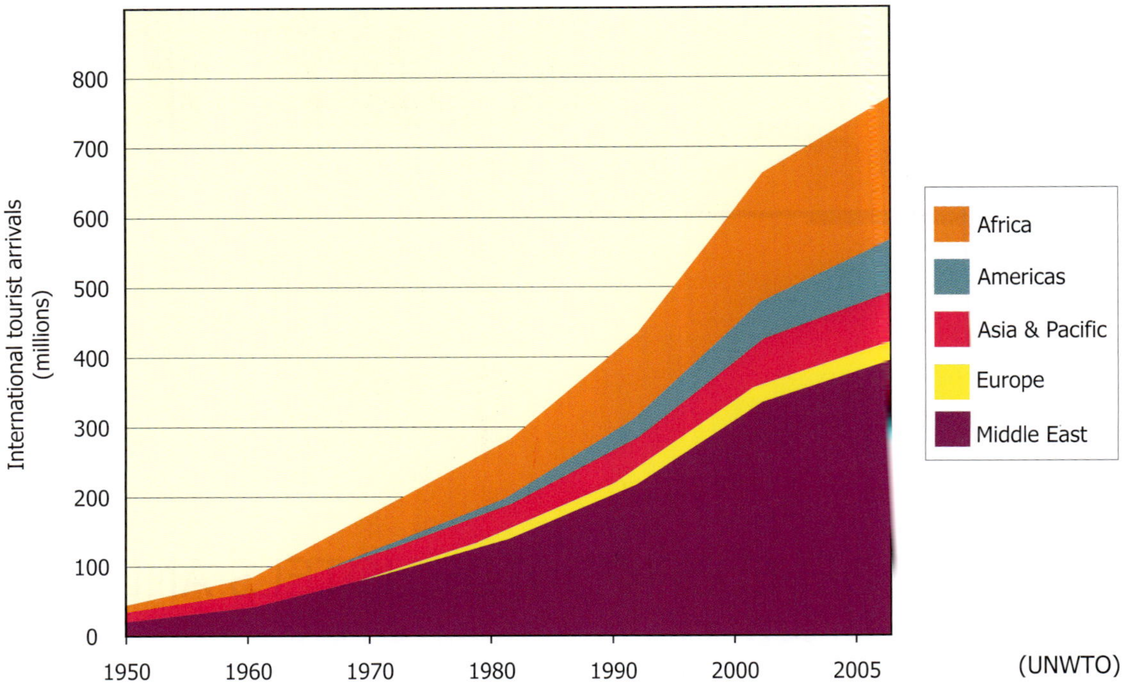

(UNWTO)

Figure 3.1: Increase in international tourism 1950–2005

	Africa	*Americas*	*Asia & Pacific*	*Europe*	*Middle East*	***World***
1950	0.5	7.5	0.2	16.8	0.2	**25.3**
1960	0.8	16.7	0.9	50.4	0.6	**69.3**
1970	2.4	42.3	6.2	113.0	1.9	**165.8**
1980	7.2	62.3	23.0	178.5	7.1	**278.1**
1990	15.2	92.8	56.2	265.5	9.6	**439.5**
2000	28.3	128.1	110.5	395.5	24.2	**687.0**
2005	37.3	133.5	155.4	441.5	39.0	**806.8**

Figure 3.2: International tourist arrivals (million) 1950–2005

ACTIVITY 1 — 15 minutes

From the data above:

Which continent received the most tourists in 1950?

Which continent was the least popular in 1950?

In 2005, which region was the most popular and which was the least popular?

What do you think has influenced the growth of tourism globally?

2 Factors influencing the industry's development

As we can see from the tables, hospitality has developed considerably; from its early days of refuges and inns for tired travellers to present-day, huge organisations servicing growing numbers of tourists, in more and more areas of the world. It's easy to equate the fact that more tourists need more accommodation. What is the hospitality industry doing to adapt to the growing demand?

A modern perspective is provided by *Gee* (1994) who explains '*the growth and success of transnational companies can be attributed to economies of scale in areas such as advertising, central reservation systems, global promotions, bulk purchasing, specialised knowledge of design and construction, and operational standardisation*'.

In section 1.1 of Chapter 2 we looked at PEST analysis. To this we will now add one further criterion: environmental. We call this STEEP analysis.

The diagram below shows the five factors that have influenced the development of the hospitality industry in recent years: Socio-Cultural, Technological, Economic, Environmental and Political; **STEEP**.

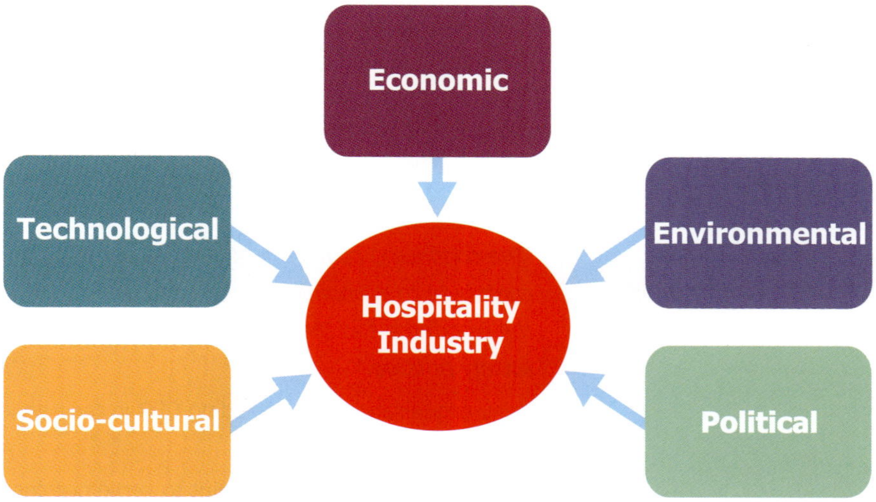

Figure 3.3: Factors influencing the industry's development

2.1 Socio-cultural factors

Hospitality development	Factor
Concessions/facilities	In Western Europe and elsewhere in the world, there is a high percentage of older people, an 'ageing population'. Therefore, many hotels and catering establishments are adapting to the needs of this growing population, including having facilities for elderly guests, such as ramps for wheelchairs, and separate dining times and activities.
Budget hotels	In recent years there has been an increase in accommodation offering low-priced rooms – 'budget hotels' – as more people, working longer hours and in stressful jobs, are taking short breaks more regularly. Many chains have developed 'budget brands' for this short-break market. Some examples are shown overleaf.
Choice of restaurants/ menus	Consumers are more exotic in their taste for different cuisines, and are therefore more demanding when it comes to dining experiences. Hotels must accommodate the wider gastronomic tastes of their guests.
Spas, gyms, resorts	People are more aware of the benefits of keeping fit and healthy, and when they are staying in a hotel, for leisure or business, like to have the facilities to exercise or relax.

Hospitality development	Factor
Room facilities	Consumers expect technological items in their rooms, due to busier lives, and higher expectations, therefore hotels must provide more advanced facilities as part of their product. This can include: flat screen TVs, DVD players and Internet access.
Locations	The locations of hotels have changed in recent times. There is still a great need for hotels in city centres, near tourist attractions, and next to airports, but there has been an increase in out-of-town hotels in more rural locations. These 'country house hotels' or resorts have developed due to consumers (in particular, business persons) demanding locations that are more relaxing and have facilities such as golf courses and spas, which generally require more land.
Total Quality Management (TQM)	Due to increased customer expectations and perceptions as to what constitutes quality, many hotels have had to raise the standard of their product. This has led to many hotels setting quality standards, such as TQM, which ensures that all aspects of the hotel operation has established standards of quality and procedures in place to ensure they are met. Other examples of quality schemes adopted by hotels include Hospitality Assured, Investors in People and ISO schemes.
Corporate Social Responsibility (CSR)	*'The continuing commitment by business to behave ethically and contribute to economic development while improving the quality of life of the workforce and their families as well as of the local community and society at large.'* (World Business Council) Many organisations are including CSR in their philosophies, and this is true in the hospitality industry. Marriott, for example in its 'spirit to serve our communities', helps communities with: ▪ Shelter and food ▪ Employment ▪ Diversity ▪ The environment ▪ Impoverished children ▪ Ethical business

Examples of budget hotels

2.2 Technological factors

Hospitality development	Factor
Computer Reservation Systems (CRS)	In today's fast-moving and increasingly competitive market, hospitality organisations are always looking at different ways in which they can provide a faster, higher quality service to secure (competitive advantage) and increase profits. Therefore in the 1990s, the hospitality industry developed CRS systems (Amadeus, Galileo, Sabre), in association with airlines, visitor attractions and reservations, 'to offer a global means of travel product distribution including the element of accommodation'. (*Knowles*, 1994:211)
Property Management Systems (PMS)	PMS was introduced in the industry to help 'front and back office' management functions, such as: accounting and finance, marketing, yield management, HR and procurement. PMS systems can help a hotel to be more efficient and enables communication between all the departments. One system used is 'Fidelio', which stores information about guests, including requests, number of times they have visited the property, preferences and so on. This information can then be passed to 'guest relations', room service etc, satisfying the needs and demands of guests before they even have to ask!
Point of Sale (POS)	Organisations are continually looking to increase profits. Many organisations now feature Point of Sales. These systems are located front and back of house in revenue-generating departments and improve communication, efficiency and control.
Energy Management Systems (EMS)	In striving to become more environmentally aware many large hotel chains now have energy management systems. These computerised systems assist in reducing energy consumption in areas throughout the hotel.
Electronic Locking System (ELS)	Many hotels nowadays feature hotel rooms with electronic locks replacing the old style key hole. Customers receive a flexible plastic card (credit card size) on check-in and this is used to access the room.

A Point of Sale terminal (POS)

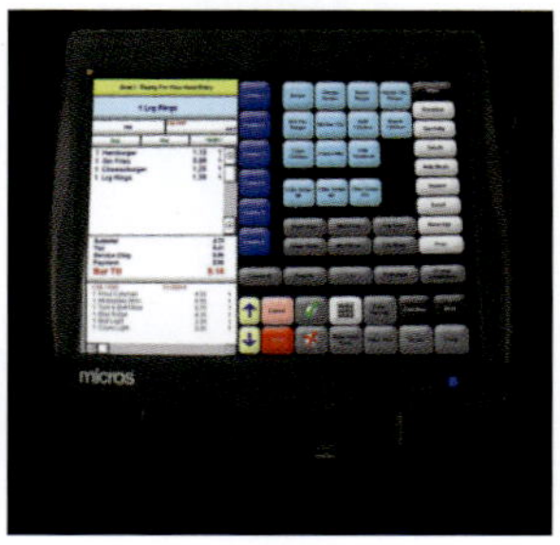

2.2.1 Yield management

Technology and sound systems can help hotels forecast more efficiently and so use their resources to the best advantage.

DEFINITION

Yeoman and Ingold (2000:3) define **yield management** as 'method which can help a firm to sell the right inventory unit to the right type of customer, at the right time, and for the right price'. (*Baker et al.,* 1994). It is composed of a set of demand-forecasting techniques used to determine whether room rates should be raised or lowered and whether a reservation should be accepted or rejected in order to maximise revenue.

As shown in the following diagram Revenue/Yield management is based on supply and demand. Prices tend to rise when demand exceeds supply; conversely, prices tend to fall when supply exceeds demand.

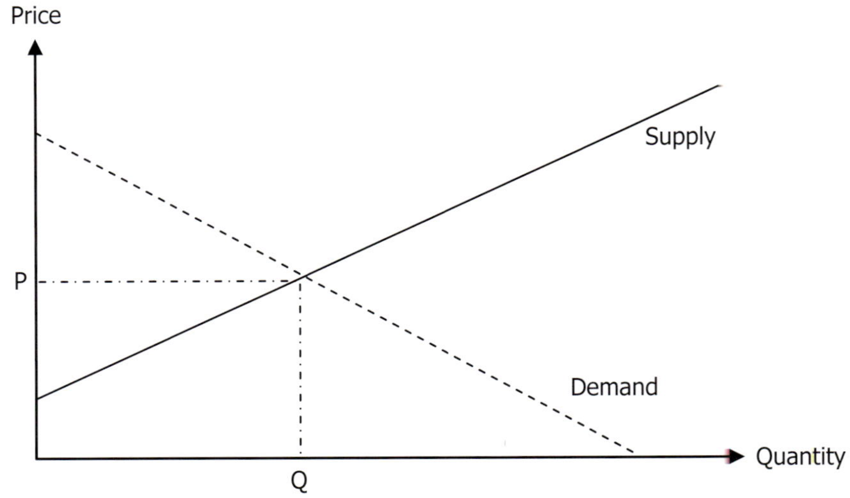

Figure 3.4: Revenue/yield

Hotels adopt yield management strategies and tactics that include:

- Restrictions
- Low demand tactics
- Pricing tactics
- High demand tactics

High and low demand tactics are how the hotel should respond during high and low demand days. High room demand can be generated in a hotel by different events as detailed in the diagram below.

School holidays	**Cultural activities, eg, pop concerts and festivals**	**Public holidays**	**Competitors' high occupancies may result in the overflow opportunities**
Religious holidays	**In-house meetings and events**	**External conferences and exhibitions**	**Local sporting events**

Extreme weather leading to transport cancellations

Demand strategies adopted by hotels

On *high* demand days	On *low* demand days
Always ..... ▪ Require minimum stays (MLOS) ▪ Raise rates ▪ Sell to groups that book meeting space and use food and beverage service ▪ Move price-sensitive groups to low demand days ▪ Tighten guarantee and cancellation policies ▪ Reduce group room allocations ▪ Consider increasing package rates ▪ Apply full price to suites and executive rooms Do not...! ▪ Accept corporate account bookings ▪ Offer discounts or promotions ▪ Accept low rate groups ▪ Provide familiarisation trips (complimentary trips to travel agents, for example) ▪ Accept non-guaranteed bookings ▪ Provide complimentary rooms of any kind ▪ Have any out of order rooms ▪ Allow any extensions or stay-overs	Always ..... ▪ Offer discounts & remove stay restrictions ▪ Provide complimentary upgrades ▪ Get employees to carry out internal QA ▪ Offer room promotions ▪ Accept group bookings ▪ Carry out deep cleaning and routine maintenance ▪ Provide familiarisation trips

ACTIVITY 2 **Homework**

Look up local events in your area and consider which days for the forthcoming year may be (a) high demand days or (b) low demand days.

What other factors influence demand (eg national bank holidays, celebrations etc)?

Name two positive and negative effects of the increased use of technology in hotels.

1 ________________ 1 ________________

2 ________________ 2 ________________

2.3 Economic factors

Hospitality development	Factor
Boutique hotels	In recent years there has been an increase in these types of hotels, which are particularly attractive to younger, trendier 'thirty-somethings', who have professional careers and high disposable incomes: '*those who do not stay in boutique hotels are categorised as unfashionable and un-hip*' (*Anhar*, 2001). These types of hotels can be found in most of the major cities in the world, in particular London, Paris and New York.

2.4 Environmental factors

Hospitality development	Factor
Eco hotels and resorts	Growing environmental awareness has led to some companies developing hotels, resorts and lodges to target consumers who care about the environment. These operations are environmentally-caring in their development, their operations and everything they do.
Recycling	Environmental regulations have been introduced to reduce the impact companies have on the environment, and one initiative is recycling, in administration (paper-less systems etc) and using recycled products. The *Environmental Management for Hotels Guide* provides guidelines for hotels to be more environmentally friendly and the European Union has an 'eco-audit' which allows businesses to assess how green they are.
Taps, showers, laundry	Another initiative is reducing laundry. Many hotels advise guests, '*leave towels on the floor if you want them washed or leave them hung up if you will use them again*'. Other measures are reminders to turn off taps, room key cards which activate lights and using 'environmentally friendly' light bulbs.

ACTIVITY 3 **Homework**

Visit: ec.europa.eu/environment/emas/index_en.htm to read more about the 'European Union Eco-Audit'.

Visit: www.ihei.org, to read more about the 'International Hotels Environment Initiative'.

Visit: www.apexhotels.co.uk/environment/, and look at the ways it is being environmentally friendly.

Do any hotels in your area/city do anything similar to the Apex hotel in London?

Corporate Social Responsibility (CSR)

A growing trend is for hotels to work closer with the local community. Many hotel chains operate internationally and this CSR encourages hotel operators to show more care and consideration for the communities in which they operate. This could be in the form of using local suppliers, recruiting locally, offering training, sponsoring local sports teams and supporting local charities.

DEFINITION

Corporate Social Responsibility (CSR)

1. The belief that a company is accountable to its community: it should take into account the social, ethical, and environmental effects of its activities on its staff, physical environment and the wider community around it.
2. The continuing commitment by a business to behave ethically and contribute to economic prosperity while improving the quality of life of the workforce and their families, as well as of the local community and society at large.
3. CSR is about a business giving back to society.

Hilton in the Community is a good example of CSR
Visit: http://www.hilton-foundation.org.uk/

ACTIVITY 4 — **Homework**

In what ways can hotels **work with** the local community?

ACTIVITY 5 — **Homework**

Visit: www.marriott.com/Images/Text%20Images/US/MarriottSocialResponsibilityandCommunityEngagement.pdf, and read more about what Marriott is doing in relation to Corporate Social Responsibility (CSR).

2.5 Political factors

Hospitality development	Factor
Globalisation	In recent years there has been a huge growth of 'global brands' in the hospitality industry '*43,000 corporate operated hotels worldwide offering in the region of 5.5 million rooms'* (Worldwide Hotel Activity Report, 2007). Due to 'globalisation' and more relaxed entry into foreign markets, many multinational companies, such as Hilton and Marriott, have opened hotels in many different parts of the world.
Environment	Environmental laws have led to changes within the hospitality sector. New regulations have required hotels to modify the design of their buildings, to not build in particular environmentally-sensitive areas and examine more environmentally-friendly ways of disposing of waste.

ACTIVITY 6 — **Homework**

Investigate a hotel or catering company of your choice, and find out what developments and changes this organisation has done in relation to the STEEP factors.

CHAPTER SUMMARY

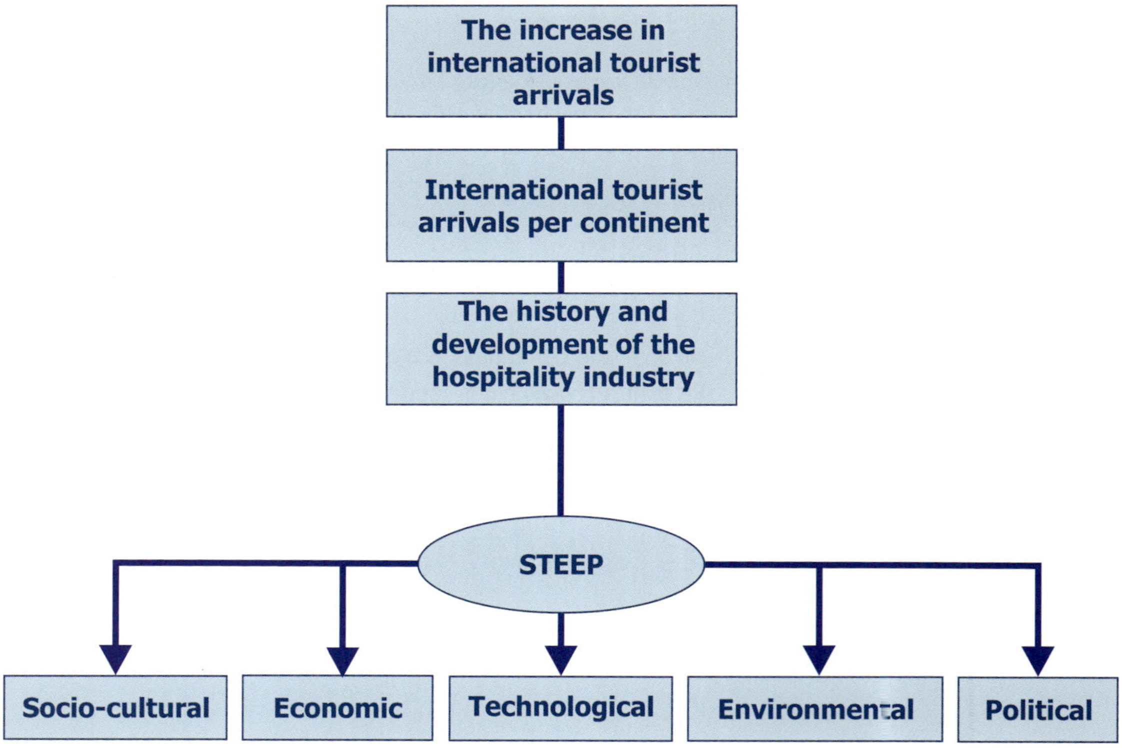

SELF-TEST QUESTIONS

1. What was the total number of international tourist arrivals in the years: 1950 and 2005?
2. In what century was the 'start of the hotel industry'?
3. In what century did technology start to make an impact on the hospitality industry?
4. What does STEEP stand for?
5. What is TQM?
6. What is CSR?
7. What does CRS mean?
8. Give an example of a PMS.

SELF-TEST ANSWERS

1. In 1950 the total number of international tourist arrivals was 25.3 million and in 2005 the total number was 806.8 million.
2. The 'start of the hotel industry' is stated as being in the 16th to 17th centuries.
3. Technology started to make an impact on the hospitality industry in the 20th century.
4. STEEP stands for: Socio-cultural, Technological, Economic, Environmental and Political.
5. TQM is Total Quality Management, and enables that certain standards are maintained throughout the whole of an organisation.
6. CSR relates to corporate social responsibility and is concerned with companies behaving ethically and contributing to economic development while improving the quality of life of the workforce and their families as well as of the local community and society at large.
7. CRS stands for Computer Reservation System and its purpose is to offer a global means of travel product distribution including the element of accommodation.
8. An example of a PMS is 'Fidelio', which stores information about guests, including requests, number of times they have visited the property and so on.

ANSWERS TO ACTIVITIES

1 The continent which received the most tourists in 1950 was Europe.

The continent which received the least number of tourists in 1950 was Asia & Pacific and the Middle-East.

In 2005 the most popular region was Europe and the least popular was Africa. The factors that have influenced the growth of tourism generally are discussed in the text that follows, in Section 2.

2 This could include public holidays, religious holidays, sporting events, cultural events or conferences/exhibitions.

Positive: For both hotel and customer – greater efficiency, cost savings, increased control (for customer), faster service, less errors

Disadvantages: For both hotel and customer – reduces contact time with customer, less personal service

For customers – Can lead to unfamiliarity in some cases, service breakdowns and a lack of personal service

3 There are no formal answers to this activity as it depends on your own research.

4

- Re-use of furniture and fittings after refurbishments by donating to local charities and businesses
- Supporting local charities
- Provide information on walks, wildlife and parks for our guests
- Use local produce for beverages, fish, meat, fruit, vegetables and dairy
- Work with local suppliers – multiplier effect
- Employ locals
- Food to homeless shelters
- Inviting local vendors to sell their products in hotel
- Promote local tourist attractions
- Monthly meetings with local residents

5 There are no formal answers to this activity as it depends on your own research.

6 There are no formal answers to this activity as it depends on your own research.

CHAPTER 4

THE GROWTH OF GLOBAL HOSPITALITY BRANDS

Chapter objectives

In this chapter you will:

- Understand the significance of global hospitality brands
- Define branding
- Identify categories of branding
- Investigate the benefits of branding
- Be introduced to global hospitality brands
- Determine hospitality globalisation strategies
- Identify the leading global hospitality brands

Topic list

1 The growth of global hospitality brands

Source: luxuo.com

Global hospitality brands have become a predominant feature of the global hospitality industry with around '*43,000 corporate operated hotels worldwide offering in the region of 5.5 million rooms*' (Worldwide Hotel Activity Report, 2007). '*In the two years from 2004 to 2006, the supply of corporate chains worldwide grew by nearly 250,000 rooms, nearly the equivalent of the chain hotel supply in France*' (*MKG Consulting*, 2007).

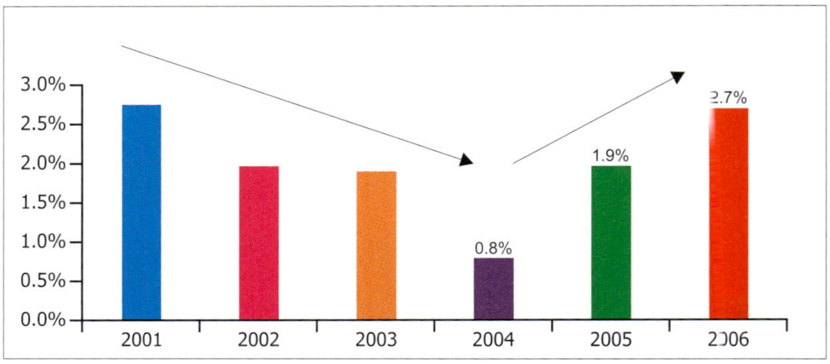

Source: MKG Consulting Database

Figure 4.1: The growth rate of the hotel supply at corporate chains worldwide from 2001 to 2006

It seems that the growing supply of rooms by the large global hospitality brands is reaping significant rewards throughout the world: '*the worldwide turnover of chains was up by 12.4% in 2006, to around 230 billion dollars, a new record*' (*MKG Consulting* 2007). The gap between the top ten brands seems to be widening: '*in 2007 growth in their cumulated supply increased by nearly 100,000 rooms, up by 2.5%.*', with '*the first six posting growth in their supply by more than 10,000 rooms each*' (*MKG Consulting*, 2007).

North America leads the way in terms of global hospitality brands, with 67% of the accommodation being provided by global hospitality brands (*Page & Connell*, 2006). Asia has the most growth in the corporate hotel chain supply in terms of both growth rate (+10.5%) and volume (around 60,000 additional rooms) in 2006. Europe on the other hand falls behind in terms of global hospitality supply with '*less than 25% for the entire continent*' (*MKG Consulting*, 2007).

FOR DISCUSSION

Why do you think there is such a high growth rate of global hospitality brands in Asia?

Why do you think the global hospitality brand supply is not so high in Europe?

2 Branding

DEFINITION

A **brand** is 'a name, term, sign, symbol, design or a combination of these elements that is intended to identify the goods or services of a seller and differentiate them from competitors' (*Kotler et al.*, 2006).

'A seller's promise to deliver a specific set of features, benefits and services to buyers' (*Kotler*, 2000).

ACTIVITY 1 — 15 minutes

For each of the elements of a brand, think of an appropriate example.

Brand element	Example of a brand
Name	
Term	
Design	

As *Scott Davis* (author of *Brand Asset Management*) highlights, '*brands are among a company's most valuable assets*' (*Kotler et al.*, 2006:316), and '*have an emotional appeal, evoking trust, quality and reliability*' (*Page & Connell*, 2006:334).

Aaker (1996) identifies four 'key assets' of a strong brand.

Brand asset	
Brand awareness	This relates to how strong a brand is in a consumer's mind, and research can be carried out to investigate the awareness of a company's brand in consumer minds.
Perceived quality	This is concerned with what consumers think about the quality of a brand. Some brand names are associated with a certain standard of quality. Consumers think if they purchase a product or service from a particular organisation, they are guaranteed a certain level of quality.
Brand loyalty	Is concerned with trying to keep and retain customers, so they do not go to competitors – 'customer defection'. Organisations may have a number of strategies they use to prevent customers purchasing competitors' products or services.
Brand associations	The value of the brand is linked to the image or identity in the minds of consumers. A brand may be associated with fun or innovation, and this same image is carried throughout all the brands of the organisation.

FOR DISCUSSION

For each of the brand assets (awareness, perceived quality, loyalty and associations), think of an organisation that excels, and how you think they achieve this.

ACTIVITY 2 — 15 minutes

Illustrated below are a selection of hotel logos.

- Write down the hotel that each logo belongs to.
- Consider why you may be familiar with some logos and not others.

2.1 Categories of branding

Brand	Description
Family brands	Each of the company's products has the same brand name. Many hotel companies have a family name, eg Holiday Inn, and each branded chain is designed to attract different segments of the market.
Individual brands	These are brands offered by a company, but with different brand names, again focused on different segments of the market.
Own-brands	These are an organisation's own brand products, which use the organisation's name and symbols.

ACTIVITY 3 — 10 minutes

For each of the categories of branding, listed above, can you think of appropriate examples from the hospitality industry.

Brand category
Family
Individual
Own-brands

2.2 Benefits of branding

- **Charge a premium price** – Branding allows organisations to charge a premium price over equivalent offers from rival companies, if the brand is easily recognised and certain attributes and characteristics can be associated with it, such as quality, reliability or innovation.
- **The ability to gain market share against rivals** – a strong brand, linked to good quality and reliability, can attract more customers and enable the organisation to sell more product, therefore gaining new customers and more market share.
- **Brand loyalty** – loyalty is concerned with the ability to keep customers, and discourage them from purchasing competitors' products or services. Brand loyalty can be achieved by the quality of the products available or by offering customers incentives to continue buying the product or service.
- **Identify with the product** – Consumers can identify with the product or service by clever branding. This can be achieved with the use of a particular logo, slogan or design, but image sometimes has to change to keep up with the times and changing demographics of the market.
- **Create an image of the product or service** – a brand can help target different segments of the market, many organisations use different brands to wider their customer base. For example, some brands may be associated with being young, exciting and fun, whereas other brands may be associated with luxury and prestige.
- **Differentiate from competitors** – A logo, symbol or trademark can help an organisation to differentiate itself from other organisations, and through this visual image it is conveyed to the consumer that the organisation has products or services to offer that may be different or superior in their quality, or lower in price.

(*Sangster*, 2000; *Page & Connell*, 2006)

FOR DISCUSSION

Think about the products or services that you buy.

When buying a product or service, what is important to you?

Do you always buy products or services from the same company?

If yes, why do you always buy products or services from this company or of this brand?

If no, why do you change the brand when buying a product or service?

3 Global hospitality brands

As the introduction to this chapter shows, the hospitality sector has increased considerably in recent years '*the WTO estimate that there are over 17 million rooms in hotels, a growth of nearly 3 million on 1997* (*Page & Connell*, 2006:208). It is the global hospitality brands have been behind the rapid growth, '*nearly 30% of all of the world's accommodation stock being chain controlled* (*Page & Connell*, 2006:208). Further predictions state that '*by 2050, up to 60% of hotels will be affiliated to global chains*' (*Howarth & Howarth*, World Hotel Industry Report, 1988).

Global hospitality brands started when Kemmons Wilson established Holiday Inn in 1952. They now account for 67% of the accommodation in the United States (*Page & Connell*, 2006:208), and their presence in the Asian market is increasing year on year. In Europe, despite this region having the most hotel rooms in the world (*6.3 million*) (*Page & Connell*, 2006:208), just over 25% (*Page & Connell*, 2006), of the accommodation is branded.

Examples of Global Hotel Brands

WESTIN HOTELS & RESORTS	Radisson	Jumeirah
Hilton	CROWNE PLAZA HOTELS & RESORTS	MILLENNIUM HOTELS AND RESORTS
Marriott	Holiday Inn	RENAISSANCE. HOTELS · RESORTS · SUITES
Sheraton HOTELS & RESORTS	RAMADA	swissôtel Hotels & Resorts
Kempinski HOTELIERS SINCE 1897	SHANGRI-LA HOTELS and RESORTS	MANDARIN ORIENTAL THE HOTEL GROUP

Regional brands

UK	Asia	Middle East
premier travel inn	SHANGRI-LA HOTELS and RESORTS	روتانا Rotana
FORTE HOTEL GROUP	MANDARIN ORIENTAL THE HOTEL GROUP	Jumeirah
Malmaison hotels that dare to be different	ĀMAN RESORTS	SHAZA
MACDONALD HOTELS & RESORTS HOME	Dusit HOTELS & RESORTS	HABTOOR HOTELS
	nikko	

3.1 Leading global hospitality brands

Rank 07	Rank 06	Group	Country	Hotels 2007	Hotels 2006	Rooms 2007	Rooms 2006	Change Rooms	Change %
1	*1*	INTERCONTINENTAL HG	GB	3,741	3,606	556,246	537,533	18,713	3.5%
2	*2*	WYNDHAM WORLDWIDE	USA	6,473	6,348	543,237	532,669	10,568	2.0%
3	*3*	MARRIOTT INT	USA	2,775	2,672	502,089	485,979	16,110	3.3%
4	*4*	HILTON CORP	USA	2,901	2,744	497,738	472,510	25,228	5.3%
5	*5*	ACCOR	FRA	4,121	4,065	486,512	475,433	11,079	2.3%
6	*6*	CHOICE	USA	5,316	5,145	429,401	418,488	10,913	2.6%
7	*7*	BEST WESTERN	USA	4,164	4,195	315,401	315,875	–474	–0.2%
8	*8*	STARWOOD HOT. & RES.	USA	871	845	265,598	257,889	7,709	3.0%
9	*9*	CARLSON HOSPITALITY	USA	945	932	145,933	146,785	–852	–0.6%
10	*10*	GLOBAL HYATT	USA	733	738	141,011	144,671	–3,660	–2.5%
		TOTAL		**32,042**	**31,302**	**3,883,369**	**3,787,832**	**95,537**	**2.5%**

Table 1 – Source: MKG Consulting Database – copyright 2006/07

ACTIVITY 4 **Homework**

Choose one of the groups or brands, and find out more information about the organisation, such as the brand logo, colours they use, how many hotels they have, how many staff they have, the locations of their hotels.

Top 20 hotel brands worldwide as at 1 January 2007

Rank 07	Rank 06	Chain	Group	Hotels 2007	Rooms 2007	Change Rooms	Change %
1	*1*	BEST WESTERN	BEST WESTERN	4,164	315,401	–474	–0.2%
2	*2*	HOLIDAY INN	INTERCONTINENTAL HG	1,395	260,470	–7,346	2.7%
3	*3*	MARRIOTT	MARRIOTT INT.	537	190,431	6,976	3.8%
4	*4*	COMFORT	CHOICE	2,439	184,716	2,243	1.2%
5	*5*	HILTON	HILTON CORP.	498	172,605	7,439	4.5%
6	*6*	DAYS INN OF AMERICA	WYNDHAM WORLD	1,859	151,438	1,136	0.8%
7	*9*	EXPRESS BY HI	INTERCONTINENTAL HG	1,686	143,582	10,028	7.5%
8	*7*	HAMPTON INN	HILTON CORP	1,392	138,487	4,366	3.3%
9	*8*	SHERATON	STARWOOD	396	135,859	1,852	1.4%
10	*10*	SUPER 8 MOTELS	WYNDHAM WORLD	2,054	126,175	2,144	1.7%
11	*12*	QUALITY	CHOICE	1,128	112,173	6,383	6.0%
12	*11*	RAMADA WORLDWIDE	WYNDHAM WORLD	871	105,986	–2,951	–2.7%
13	*13*	COURTYARD	MARRIOTT INT.	733	105,526	5,857	5.9%
14	*16*	MOTEL 6	ACCOR	928	95,628	1,682	1.8%
15	*15*	HYATT HOTELS	GLOBAL HYATT	214	94,224	–921	–1.0%
16	*17*	MERCURE	ACCOR	732	89,624	2,391	2.7%
17	*14*	RADISSON HOTELS	CARLSON HOSP	400	89,365	–5,335	–5.6%
18	*18*	IBIS	ACCOR	745	82,546	3,766	4.8%
19	*20*	CROWNE PLAZA	INTERCONTINENTAL HG	275	75,632	10,228	15.6%
20	*19*	NOVOTEL	ACCOR	397	70,373	1,118	1.6%
		TOTAL		**22,843**	**2,740,241**	**50,582**	**1.9%**

Table 2 – Source: MKG Consulting Database – copyright 2006/07

The two tables above show the leading hotel brands for the year 2007. Table 1, lists the global hospitality groups and the number of hotels and rooms for the years 2006 and 2007. It also shows the percentage change in the number of rooms for the brand, from 2006 to 2007. Table 2 details the individuals' 'chains', or brand for each of the different hospitality groups.

ACTIVITY 5 — 5 minutes

Looking at the first table, match the chains or brands with their corresponding hotel group.

Hospitality group	Chain/brand

FOR DISCUSSION

Which hotel groups and brands (chains) do you recognise?

Are any of the brands located in the area or city where you live?

Are there any other hotel brands in your local area or region?

Are they owned by companies from your country?

ACTIVITY 6 — 45 minutes

Holiday Inn hotels was one of the first hotel brands. Recently the chain launched a new logo, changing its brand image. Discuss

- Why would a chain re-brand?
- What are the challenges and opportunities?
- What are the risks?

Multinational hotel group development

Branding and globalisation has developed simultaneously. Many hotel chains have developed their brands overseas through different strategies. However, this development comes with both opportunities and challenges for the hotel operators.

Opportunities

According to *Gee* (1994) some of the reasons that domestic project developers and hotel operators look beyond their own borders for expansion opportunities include potential new markets, capital availability, cheap and abundant labour, the rise and growth of global tourism, and tax incentives.

Challenges

Gee continues: *'the opportunities for growth and increased market share may be considerable in the international marketplace, but global expansion is not without its drawbacks. It is seldom marked by immediate profitability and success when measured against domestic standards. Nationalism, cultural differences, and the lack of adequate supplies may result in recurrent problems with resource availability, compromised quality and consistency standards, and runaway costs which often plague foreign operators. On a more day-to-day basis problems can be caused due to geographic distance and time differences with the host operator'.*

3.2 Hospitality globalisation strategies

Athiyaman and Go (2003:143) cited in *Brotherton* (2003):

> *'The forms of concentrated growth are strategic alliances, franchising, management contracts, joint ventures and acquisition. Strategic alliances are common in the international hospitality industry.*
>
> *Many, if not most international hospitality firms have one or more strategic partnerships with other hotel chains and increasingly with synergistically related organisations such as car rental organisations, airlines and life insurance companies.'*

We look at these below.

DEFINITION

Franchising – *'hotels and motels are operated by individual franchisees (proprietors) paying royalties to the parent company for the privilege of operating under a brand name'* (*Holloway*, 2006:273). This type of operation is very popular in other businesses in other countries.

Athiyaman and Go (2003:143) cited in *Brotherton* (2003):

> *'Franchising is one of the most common and preferred forms of expansion for international hospitality firms. It is linked to the proliferation of branding that is evident in the international hospitality industry.*
>
> *The franchise method can be either applied to licensing a single franchisee or a master licence that gives the franchisee the right to open an agreed number of units within a particular geographic area.'*

Franchise agreement

As an example of franchising, we use McDonald's to explain and evaluate the concept.

Evaluation of franchise agreement: McDonald's and franchisee

Opportunities for organisation (McDonald's)	▪ Vehicle to expand company ▪ Expansion of the chain ▪ Financial growth ▪ Brand expansion and growth ▪ Guaranteed monthly fees ▪ Less capital investment in infrastructure ▪ Less responsibility for expenditure ▪ Less accountability
Challenges for McDonald's	▪ Potential loss of control ▪ Franchisee unable to maintain standards ▪ Closer monitoring ▪ Loss of standards may result in dissatisfied customers switching loyalty ▪ One poor franchisee damages good franchisees

Opportunities for franchisee (Mr X)	▪ Purchases well-known brand, recognised name ▪ Established customer base ▪ Employee training programme is provided by McDonald's ▪ Assistance with set-up to include instructions, guidelines and technical know–how ▪ Financial advice and assistance provided ▪ Established standards and procedures ▪ Access to mass media marketing and Public Relations (PR) ▪ Low failure rate
Challenges for franchisee	▪ High start-up costs ▪ Need to share profit ▪ Strict terms and conditions ▪ Franchisees have limited negotiation power in terms of benefits or franchise fees ▪ Management regulation and control ▪ One weak unit can affect all units ▪ Have to pay company monthly fees irrespective of economic climate ▪ Limited flexibility – lots of standardisation ▪ Hard to respond quickly to changes in external environment

Examples of restaurant franchises

Management contracting

DEFINITION

Management contracting is when an owner or operator of an establishment employs or contracts a specialised hospitality or food and beverage service company to manage the whole or part of the operation. This could be done either in a hotel or in a non- commercial institution, for example a university.

Athiyaman and Go (2003:143) cited in *Brotherton* (2003):

> *'Management contracts have also become an increasingly popular means of hotel operation. Through a legal agreement, the management contract, it enables the owner to employ an operator to assume full responsibility for the professional management of the property. Four Seasons Hotels, Hyatt International and InterContinental are examples of successful hotel management contract companies.'*

EXAMPLE

Hilton Hotels has been used to explain the concept of management contracting.

Management contracting analysis

Opportunities for owner, Mr X	▪ Hotel operator brings experience and expertise ▪ An established, known brand ▪ Existing loyal customers ▪ Standards, systems and infrastructure ▪ Centralised reservation system ▪ Less responsibility and accountability
Challenges for Mr X	▪ Little personal recognition ▪ Little or no direct involvement in management of hotel ▪ Pays monthly fees to contractor
Opportunities for hotel operator (Hilton)	▪ Little capital investment required ▪ A vehicle to expand into new markets ▪ Less financial risk ▪ Economies of scale ▪ Brand growth
Challenges for hotel operator (Hilton)	▪ Does not own property or assets ▪ Potential unwanted involvement from owner ▪ Some bureaucracy – owner approves major expenditures ▪ Owner thinks 'they are the manager!'

Typical negotiation points in management contracts

Financial provisions

- Management fees – basic, incentive, payment method
- Financial goals of owner
- Responsibility for capital improvement, repairs
- Reserve for replacement/substitution of furniture, fixtures and equipment
- Preparation of budgets, plans
- Working capital balances
- Equity contribution and loans
- Insurance and risk protection
- Damage, destruction, compulsory taking or condemnation
- Property taxes
- Negotiation of fixed commitments
- Pre-opening budget

Administration provisions

- Books, records, and statements
- Accounting system used, frequency of reports
- Hotel personnel
- Legal and licensing requirements
- Technical services

Operations provisions

- Operating plan
- Pricing schedules
- Services provided
- Procurement
- Negotiation of service contracts
- Quality standards/inspections
- Pre-opening management services

General provisions

- Agency relationship
- Length of contract
- Owner's right of sale or assignment
- Indemnification
- Use of the hotel's company name
- Requisite approvals
- Performance requirements
- Default and termination
- Governing law of host country and arbitration

Marketing provisions

- Marketing, advertising, and promotions
- Reservation systems and services

Source: *Gee* (1994)

ACTIVITY 7 **30 minutes**

Consider the following:

- You are a businessman and have a planned a meeting with a potential hotel operator to run your hotel investment, draft a list of questions you would ask.
- You are a hotel management company and are about to meet a businessman who has an interest in you to run his hotel, draft a list of questions you would ask.

Strategic alliances

DEFINITION

Johnson et al (2008:362) explain that **strategic alliances** is 'where two or more organisations share resources and activities'.

Examples of hotel companies that have formed alliances are Regent with Four Seasons and Raffles with Swissotel. Both Regent and Raffles were Far Eastern-based hotels chains with little presence in Euope. Similarly, Four Seasons and Swissotel had little hotel presence in the Far East. By forming a strategic partnership they were able to obtain brand recognition on different continents, share resources to exploit economies of scale, gain market share and ultimately achieve higher revenues.

Another type of strategic alliance is the collaboration between airlines and hotel companies.

Gee (1994) explains *'many airlines would develop or acquire their own hotels as a way of ensuring that their passengers and their flight crews had somewhere to sleep. Benefits of linkages with airlines include cross-marketing, reservation system linkage, promotional tie ins and frequent flyer promotions'.*

They are many examples of alliances between airlines and hotel franchises.

Airline	Hotel chain
British Airways	Pan Pacific Hotels
Singapore Airlines	Jumeirah Hotels
Quantas	Accor
Etihad	Rendezvous Hotels & Resorts
United Airlines	Westin Hotels & Resorts
Emirates Airlines	Taj Group of Hotels

Other forms of strategic alliance

Acquiring overseas properties/interests – referred to as 'integration'. In particular horizontal integration, '*where an organisation takes ownership of another organisation*' (*Johnson et al.*, 2008:356), means one organisation buys, and then controls, another organisation.

Licensing – other companies are given a licence to operate under an organisation's brand, logo or trademark.

Mergers – '*a mutually agreed decision for joint ownership*' (*Johnson et al.*, 2008:357) is another example of 'horizontal integration' and can enable an organisation to penetrate markets in a number of countries.

Consortia – is similar to a joint venture, but it is a joining together of two or more organisations for a particular project. It is common for independent properties to join consortia, such as 'The Leading Hotels of the World'.

The Leading Hotels of the World

Benefits of joining consortia

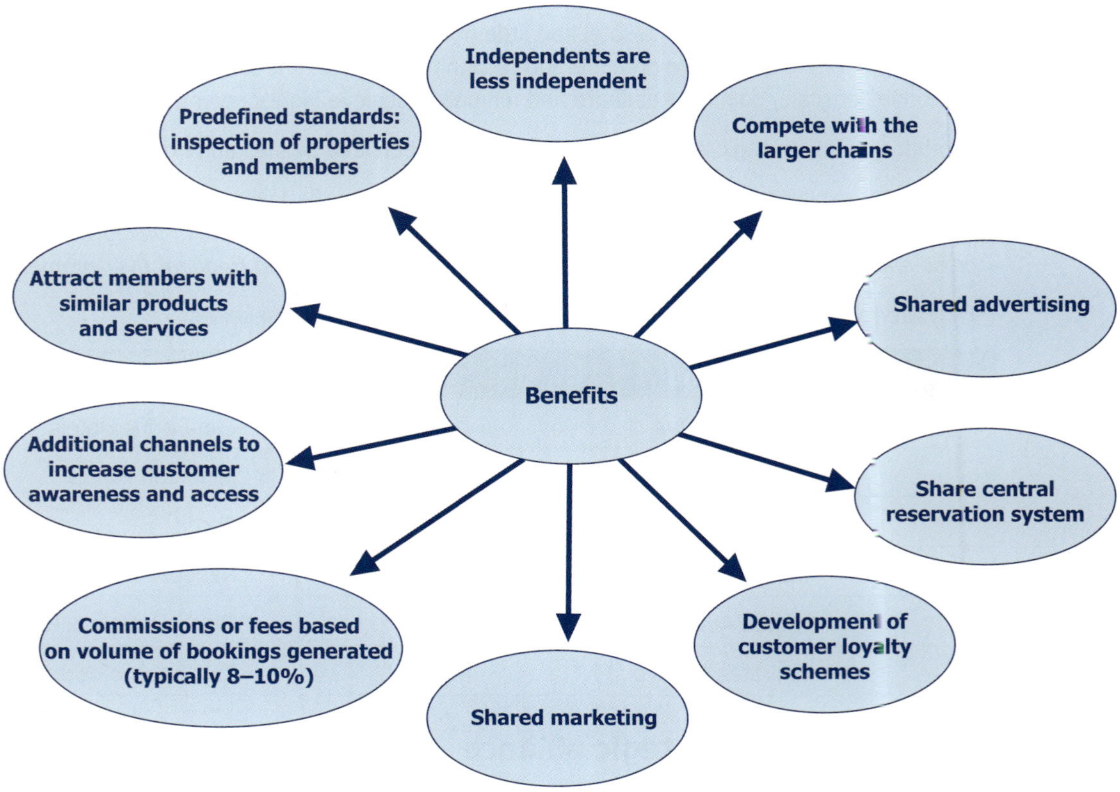

Source: BHA Statistics

Figure 4.2: UK Hotel Marketing Consortia (2007)

Consortia	Hotels in UK	No of rooms in UK
Best Western	290	15,500+
The Independents Hotel Association	180+	11,000+
The Circle	450+	5,500+
Classic British Hotels	50+	3,362+
Leading Hotels of the World	17	2,850+
Great Hotels Organisation	18	1,832
Small Luxury hotels	35	1,749
Pride of Britain	32	1,040
Design Hotels	12	875
Preferred Hotels and Resorts	5	567
Relais and Chateaux	23	500
Concorde Hotels	1	416
Minotel	5	233

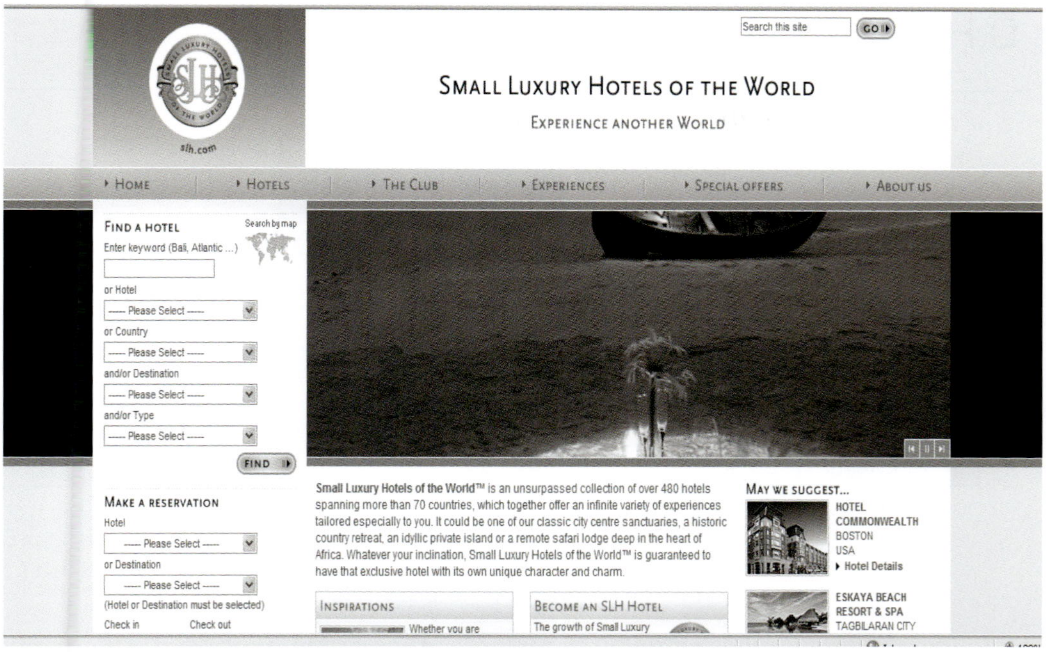

FOR DISCUSSION

Why do you think many global hospitality brands use these different 'globalisation' strategies?

Independent hotels and restaurants

What are the impacts for SMEs?

Go and Appelman (2001) in *Brotherton* (2003):

'The rise of mass individualisation offers SMEs a great opportunity to add value through differentiated production and marketing. In general, small business hospitality operators have little, if any awareness of global standards. However, hospitality has the potential to serve as a change agent due to its function of connecting host and guest.'

CHAPTER SUMMARY

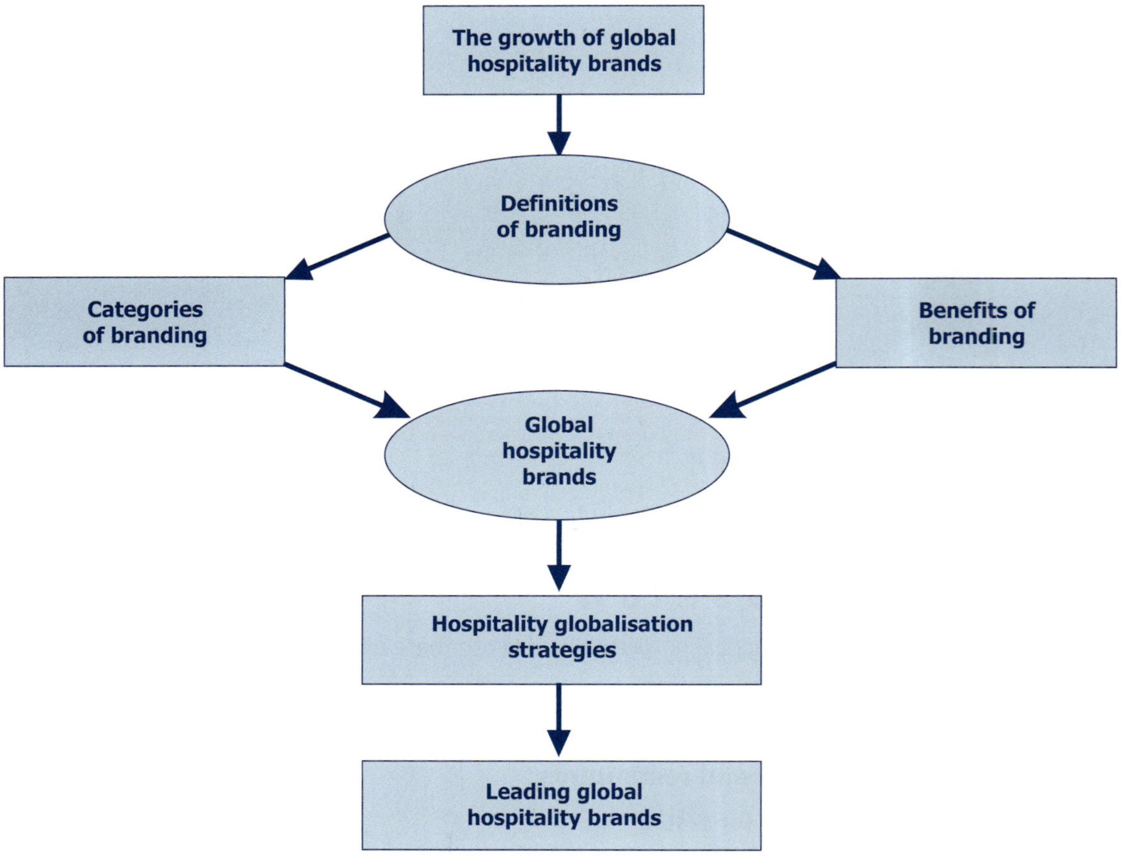

SELF-TEST QUESTIONS

1. According to the Worldwide Hotel Activity Report (2007), how many hotels in the world are corporate operated?
2. Which continent has the most hotels operated by global hospitality brands? And what is the percentage?
3. Give a definition of branding.
4. What are the five elements of a brand?
5. According to *Aaker* (1996) there are four 'key assets' of a strong brand. What are they?
6. Identify and explain the categories of branding.
7. Identify the benefits of branding.
8. List the hospitality globalisation strategies.
9. Identify the top ten leading global hospitality brands.

SELF-TEST ANSWERS

1. According to the Worldwide Hotel Activity Report (2007) 43,000 hotels throughout the world are corporate operated, offering in the region of 5.5 million rooms.

2. North America has the most number of hotels operated by global hospitality brands, with 67% being operated by global hospitality brands.

3. According to *Kotler* (2006), a brand is '*a name, term, sign, symbol, design or a combination of these elements that is intended to identify the goods or services of a seller and differentiate them from competitors*'.

4. The five elements of a brand are: name, term, sign, symbol and design.

5. According to *Aaker* (1996) the four 'key assets' of a strong brand are: Brand awareness, perceived quality, brand loyalty and brand associations.

6. The categories of branding are: family brands, individual and own brands.

   Family brands are when each of the company's products has the same brand name, and each branded chain is designed to attract different segments of the market.

   Individual brands are brands offered by a company, but with different brand names, focusing on different segments of the market.

   Own brands are products, which use the organisation's name and symbols.

7. The benefits of branding are: charge a premium price, gain market share against rivals, brand loyalty, identify with the product and create an image of the product or service.

8. Globalisation strategies in hospitality are: franchising, licensing, strategic alliances, acquisitions and mergers.

9. The top ten leading global hospitality brands are:

   - InterContinental
   - Wyndham Worldwide
   - Marriott Int
   - Hilton Corp
   - Accor
   - Choice
   - Best Western
   - Starwood Hotels and Resorts
   - Carlson Hospitality
   - Global Hyatt

ANSWERS TO ACTIVITIES

1

Brand element	Example of a brand
Name	Hilton
Term	'Travel should take you places'
Design	Marriott has the colour maroon on all its products, websites etc

2

Some logos may be more familiar as:

- They are larger chains and have global representation
- Some chains are more prominent in TV advertising than others
- Some hotels have been established for many years and others have not
- Some hotels are located near home, study or work

3 **Family brands** – Holiday Inn Express – uses the family name, but are hotels mainly located in city centres or near airports, for short stay guests.

Individual brands – Courtyard – a brand name used by Marriott for a budget hotel brand in its group.

Own brands – Marriott – has many different brands for different market segments and also owns hotels which are run as franchises.

4 There are no formal answers to this activity as it depends on your own research.

5

Hospitality group	Chain/brand
Accor	Ibis, Mercure, Motel 6, Novotel
Best Western	Best Western
Carlson Hospitality	Radisson Hotels
Choice	Comfort, Quality
Global Hyatt	Hyatt Hotels
Hilton	Hampton Inn, Hilton
InterContinental	Crowne Plaza, Express by Holiday Inn, Holiday Inn
Marriott	Courtyard, Marriott
Starwood Hotel and Resorts	Sheraton
Wyndham Worldwide	Days Inn of America, Super 8 Motels, Ramada Worldwide

6 Holiday Inn is a very established hotel chain with a well recognised brand. However, after such a long time the company decided to refresh its brand image. A hugely expensive exercise, it is undertaken to ensure the chain remains competitive and to convey key messages about the company's ability to change to customers.

Challenges – For a global brand with many properties the costs involved are vast. Signage, advertising boards, in-house literature and websites all have to be updated.

Opportunities – To be competitive, attract new customers and retain existing customers.

The risk is that customers who are familiar with the old brand don't recognise the new brand image and logo or it doesn't appeal to them.

7

1 Contractual details such as commission, duration, terms and conditions
2 Level of experience in current market
3 Level of experience in managing hotels for individuals and how successful, track record
4 Testimonials from other owners
5 Can they guarantee 100% quality and customer satisfaction?
6 Time for return on investment
7 Financial stability of company

1 Contractual details such as commission, duration, terms and conditions
2 Financial stability
3 Objectives for the hotel
4 Experience with working with other contractors
5 Testimonials from other contractors

CHAPTER 5

THE ACCOMMODATION INDUSTRY

Chapter objectives

In this chapter you will:

- Describe the considerations when planning a hotel
- Be introduced to the accommodation sector
- Discover the different accommodation types
- Investigate the significance of each of the accommodation types
- Be introduced to different distribution systems

Topic list

1 Hotel development

1.1 Hotel location decisions

Before looking at the different types of accommodation, we should consider the key considerations for hotel development. This is not an exhaustive list. The variables change depending on whether the project is a new development or taking over an existing hotel facility or property.

Source: www.copypoint.ca/images/blueprint.jpg

Considerations in hotel development

Management method	Land costs	Local competition	P Marketing Mix
Infrastructure	Budget	Sales plan	Breakeven analysis
Labour resources	Suppliers and support	Environment assessment	Target markets
Local culture	PESTLE	Market feasibility study	

Management method

Hoteliers have a choice in relation to how the property will be managed. This could include:

- Self-managed and owned by the hotel
- Management contract
- Franchise (in most cases, for budget level properties)
- Outsourced from another specialised company

PESTLE	Political, Economic, Social, Technological, Legal and Environmental. Follows on from PEST and STEEP analysis. Macro-environmental factors that need research prior to the development of the hotel. If, for example, the destination is experiencing political unrest or economic instability this may deter hotel developers from investing there.
Land costs	Land costs will impact both on purchasing or renting the property. This will determine the size and allocation of space, particularly the balance between leisure areas, food and beverage service and accommodation.
Competition	Some academics say that it is not good to be the first or the last to enter a location. However, if the product is good it can be successful. A full analysis of the competition is required prior to developing a hotel to ensure differentiation in one or more of the following areas: ■ Product ■ Service ■ Facilities ■ Price
P marketing mix	In considering the area decisions on the most suitable Product, Price, People, Place and Promotion need to be taken. **Product** – the physical product, design, branding, standards, aesthetic characteristics. Many multinational companies now consider the local environment. According to *Gee* (1994) the slogan for the 1990s was 'think globally, act locally', striking the balance between a global perspective and local markets needs and desires. **Price** – what is the correct price to set for products in relation to targets, customers and competitors? *Buttle* (1986) defines price as: *'The summation of all sacrifices made by the consumer in order to experience the benefits of the product.'* **People** – qualified, skilled employees delivering consistent service **Place** – how will the products be delivered? For example, travel agents, central reservation system, Internet **Promotion** – methods the hotel will adopt to promote the property and its facilities to its target market
Infrastructure	The underlying framework of facilities and systems, for example, water, electricity, gas, transportation and communication systems.
Budget	A budget is a plan of forecasted revenue and expenses to assist managers in achieving targets.
Sales plan	The sales plan a company's the budget detailing how forecasted revenues will be achieved.
Breakeven analysis	How long it will take for the property to break even financially?
Target markets	A clear plan of who the target markets are, how to meet their needs, how to reach, attract and retain them.
Labour resources	Staffing is such an important element of hospitality. Operators must consider the availability of skilled labour in the destination.
Suppliers and support	The operator needs to ensure that that there are good suppliers available who can offer quality products, reliably, and at competitive prices. Support for facilities is also critical to ensure that customers and employees are provided with a fully functional environment.

Environmental assessment	Today new hotel developers will employ a specialist to carry out an Environmental Impact Assessment to determine how the development of a hotel may impact the local area environmentally.
Culture	For developments overseas hotel operators should consider local culture and incorporate this into product design and service.
Market feasibility study	*Gee* (1994) explains a feasibility study should include: ▪ A detailed analysis of potential demand for the project (broken down by different segments) ▪ An analysis of supply factors such as existing and proposed properties in the area ▪ Detailed financial projections usually forecasted ten years from the estimated opening date

2 Accommodation

Accommodation is extremely important for every destination whatever the size. Some tourists want to stay overnight. Excursionists, 'day trippers', do not require overnight accommodation. Accommodation is of more significance for 'international tourists', or 'domestic tourists' who have travelled for long distances.

Depending on the size and dynamic of the destination, there are a number of different accommodation types which may be appropriate.

2.1 Accommodation types

Generally, accommodation falls into two types:

- Catered (serviced)
- Self-catered (non-serviced)

Catered	Self-catered
Hotels Formal accommodation offering full services. These can include: 'country house hotels' with big gardens set in the countryside or a 'metro hotel' which can be found in a city centre.	**Apartments and villas** Privately-owned by individuals or companies, where the guests provide their own food and do their own cooking
Guesthouses Accommodation for more than six paying guests, with the owner and staff providing more services, for example, dinner.	**Campus accommodation** University halls of residences, where tourists can rent rooms, during non-term time.
Bed and breakfast (B&B) Accommodation provided in a private house by the owner for up to six paying guests.	**Youth hostel** Generally basic accommodation, where guests stay in dormitories or rooms with other people and kitchen facilities are provided.
Farmhouses B&B or Guesthouse accommodation provided on a working farm.	**Camp sites** Privately-owned land, where tourists pay a nightly-fee to pitch their tent or caravan, with washing facilities and electricity sometimes provided.

Other accommodation

Time-share – tourists pay for access to an apartment for a set date over a number of years.

Accommodation in other countries

Gee (1994) points out some other types of accommodation that can be found in different countries.

Spain – Paradors – historic buildings such as castles, palaces, convents and monasteries converted into hotels and operated by the State.

Portugal – 45% of visitors to Portugal stay in Pensions, or guesthouses, while others stay in hotels and State-operated inns known locally as Pousadas.

Japan – Ryokan – traditional small guesthouses with tatami mats and landscaped gardens. Capsule hotels can also be found in Japan, mostly in cities and offer a very small space to sleep.

A capsule hotel

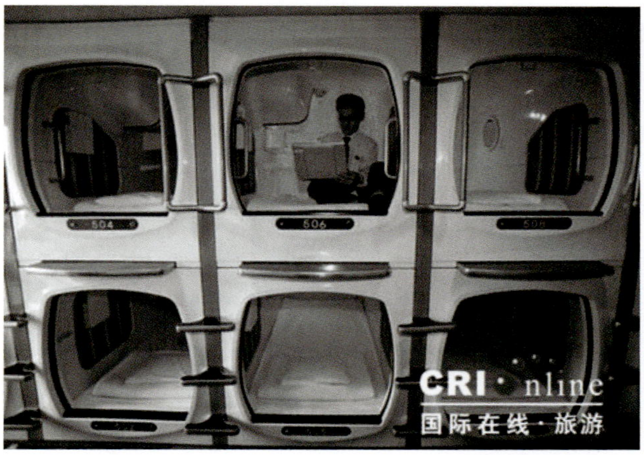

Source: travellingboard.net/tag/tokyo/

FOR DISCUSSION

What do you are the most common types of accommodation in your country/region?

Why do you think these are the most popular accommodation types?

As shown, there are a number of different types of accommodation in the two catered and non-catered categories, and the demand for a particular type of accommodation relates to numerous factors, most notably the 'purpose of the journey' or motivation for travel. According to *Jones* (2002) the different sources for demand for accommodation include:

- Government officials
- Business travellers
- Leisure travellers
- Tour groups
- Conference participants
- Other users

FOR DISCUSSION

Can you think of any other users of accommodation?

Form of journey	Business	Leisure
Route	← **Airport hotels** →	
	← **Motels** →	
	← **Inns** →	
	← **State-run establishments** → eg Paradors, Spain	
		Youth accommodation ▪ Youth hostels ▪ YMCA/YWCA
Transport as tourism		**Cruise liner** **Orient Express**
Destination	← **Urban hotels** → All types of hotels for business, conferences and exhibitions	
	← **Executive residences** →	
	← **University accommodation** →	
		All-inclusives
	← **Self-catering** →	
	← **Apartment hotels** → (Aparthotel)	
		Farm stays
		Timeshare
		Caravans/camping
		Villas
		Forest villages
		Visiting friends and relatives (VFR)
		Second homes ▪ Non-mobile: cottages, houses and apartments ▪ Semi-mobile: trailers, mobile homes, tents and caravans ▪ Mobile: sailing boats, canal boats

Adapted from *Hall & Page* (1999)

Figure 5.1: Accommodation types

ACTIVITY 1 — 20 minutes

From Figure 5.1, identify:

- Which accommodation types are suitable for both business and leisure tourists?
- Which are only for leisure tourists?

FOR DISCUSSION

Which are the most popular types of accommodation in a region?

Why do you think these are the most popular types of accommodation?

2.2 Catered (serviced) accommodation

Serviced accommodation generally involves the provision of a number of services, including: food, laundry, guest services, room service, housekeeping, leisure facilities, concierge and AV services for conferences and meetings.

- Hotels
- Guesthouses
- Bed and breakfasts (B&Bs)
- Farmhouses

2.2.1 Hotels

'*The hotel is among the most visible and easily identifiable sub-sector within the accommodation business*' (*Page & Connell*, 2006:212), but there are a vast number of different types of hotel, each catering for different needs and segments of the accommodation market.

Holloway (2006:284) identifies 'the hotel product is made up of five characteristics':

- **Location**
- Its **mix of functions** (which include its bedrooms, restaurants, other public rooms, function rooms and leisure facilities)
- **Image**
- **Services** (level of formality, personal attention, speed and efficiency of its staff)
- **Price**

Business and conference hotels

Factors	Description
Hotel development and location	Business and conference hotels began to develop near areas of large economic activity, such as capital and large commercial cities like London, to satisfy the needs of the 'commercial traveller'. As times have changed, the locations of business and conference hotels has also changed 'to the peace and tranquillity of the countryside'. Therefore many hotels have been established in large country houses – 'Country House Hotels', and these rural locations provide plenty of space for more leisurely pursuits such as golf courses, swimming pools and leisure facilities to satisfy the need to relax of 'stressed-out' executives.

Factors	Description
Size and scale of the sector	Accommodation is extremely important for 'the commercial traveller', and figures show that '*66% of business travellers use hotels*' (*Jones*, 1996:38). '*Despite staying in hotels for shorter periods of time than leisure guests... 5.7 days on average*' (*Jones*, 1996:38), the revenues received by hotels from business guests is significantly higher. Business travellers are a very significant market for the hotel industry, '*two-thirds of most leading hotels' occupancy rates is accounted for by the business and conference market*' (*Jones*, 1996:39), therefore many hotels have been developed with the business and conference sector in mind. Furthermore, many large hotel chains have agreements with large companies, to provide accommodation and conferencing facilities for their staff, while they are travelling domestically and internationally on behalf of their organisation.
Markets served	**Business market** has particular needs, such as: broadband, wi-fi, express check-in, executive lounge and secretarial services. Location is very important: close proximity to a transport hub such as an airport or train station is essential. Particular in-room facilities may be provided such as trouser press, business channels on TV, IPOD docking station and business magazines. **Conference market** – divided into two: ▪ 'Day-delegate': room-hire, lunch and refreshments ▪ '24 hour': room-hire, breakfast, dinner and accommodation These facilities can also be used to host banqueting events such as weddings, festivals and other celebrations. **Airport market** – Airport and airline users market: pilots and cabin crew, travellers of delayed or cancelled flights and in-bound and out-bound passengers, who require accommodation very close to the airport, due to a long-haul flight or an early flight. These hotels situated at (or close to) airports target short stay customers and crew and can benefit from **over** 100% occupancy due to selling the same room twice in a day. **Leisure market** – Many business hotels will also accommodate leisure travellers on weekends and occasions where they need to increase occupancy. *Gee* (1994) notes '*about 40% of worldwide demand for hotel accommodation is leisure orientated*'. **Groups –** Most hotels will accommodate groups at some point. Groups can be either business, conference or leisure. When accommodating groups specific management is required in advance and during their stay to ensure customer satisfaction. This may include blocking off rooms, preparation of key cards, separate check-in and check-out areas and packages for food and beverage requirements.
Product offering	Technology is a very important factor for business travellers and hotels that can offer the latest technology (broadband, AV facilities, executive services), can use this as a unique selling point to differentiate themselves from their competitors (at least for a while!). Furthermore, the conference facilities should be of the highest standard and equipped with the latest technology. To satisfy the demands of the business and conference market, ideally a hotel should offer a number of conference rooms of different sizes.

Factors	Description
Organisation	Business hotels need to: ▪ Be co-ordinated efficiently, effectively and fast, but seamlessly ▪ Have courteous and quick responding staff ▪ Have excellent communication between all departments
Current issues and future trends	Many hotels are already using very complex Central Reservations Systems (CRS), thus enabling them to be more efficient and streamlined in maintaining occupancy levels, and these are set to develop even further. However, advances in technology can also have a negative impact on the conference and business hotels industry, in particular video-conferencing, means global conferences can be held without the need to physically travel and meet other delegates. The impact is greater now many large companies now have their own 'in-house' conference rooms with AV equipment, therefore the need to hold conferences externally is no longer a requirement.

Resort hotels

'The provision of accommodation and substantial other services at one location.' *Poon* (1998:62)

'Destinations in their own right ... completely self-contained.' *Roper, ibid Jones* (1996:50)

Source: amanresorts.com

Resort hotels

Factors	Description
Hotel development and location	Resorts were originally introduced in Europe in the 1950s, with the establishment of Butlin's Holiday villages in the UK and Club Mediterranee in France. Since then many resorts have been set-up throughout the world *'offering a basic theme activity, such as a championship golf course, with a wide range of supporting activities (from watersports to hunting)*' (*Roper, ibid Jones*, 1996:50), and '*include everything in the pre-paid price – from airport transfers, baggage handling, government taxes, rooms, all meals, snacks, drinks and use of all the facilities, equipment and certified instructors…the result is that the use of cash is eliminated*' (*Page & Connell*, 2006:215).

Factors	Description
Size and scale of the sector	In the UK there are two main types of resort hotels: ▪ **Country resort hotels** – located in peaceful, rural locations and generally on a large-scale (100 rooms or more), they offer extensive leisure and recreational facilities such as golf courses, and more recently spa facilities. The majority of the resort hotels in the UK are operated by major hotel chains such as Marriott's 'Marriott Hotel & Country Clubs'. ▪ **Holiday villages/centres** – these types of resorts offer accommodation such as apartments, villas, chalets, and are essentially self-contained villages, offering a range of leisure facilities, such as swimming pools and a range of eating outlets, such as cafes and restaurants. Popular examples includes: Butlin's and Center Parcs.
Markets served	▪ **Country resort hotels** – would be more associated with the middle to upper class segment of the market, possibly those of socio-economic groups A-C1 in terms of the leisure market and also the business and conference market as identified above. ▪ **Holiday villages/centres** – provide a product that is targeted more at the C-E groups, in particular families with younger children with limited disposable incomes.
Product offering	Generally located in rural locations, with a few exceptions (the most notable being Las Vegas where the 'basic theme activity' is gambling), resorts have enough space to offer a great number of sporting facilities, including golf courses, tennis courts and horse riding. Many have now followed a growing trend to offer spa facilities.
Organisation	Due to the emphasis and size of resorts, resorts differ in terms of staffing from a traditional hotel. Importance is placed on the sporting activities, therefore many staff members have to be physically fit and educated in the areas of sport, fitness and beautification.
Current issues and future trends	This particular type of establishment has grown considerably in recent years, as consumers take more short breaks away from their routine lives. Many countryside resorts place a great emphasis on respect for the environment, appealing to consumers' consciences. Center Parcs has won many awards for its 'green credentials' based on its policy of sustainability; once inside the village guests cannot use their cars. Generally, consumers are now very much more aware of their impact on the environment and wish to reduce their carbon footprint.

Budget hotels

<table>
<tr><th>Factors</th><th>Description</th></tr>
<tr><td>Hotel development and location</td><td>Budget hotels '2–3 star accommodation at 1–2 star tariffs' (Johnson & Clifton, ibid Jones (1996:62)) have become more numerous in recent years, due to the shift in consumer demand from B&B and small hotels to new 'low-cost', high quality accommodation. Further, many business travellers use these budget hotels – 'up to 50% of budget hotel business' (Page & Connell (2006:216)) – due to the standard features included in these types of hotels: en-suite facilities, telephone, television, and their locations. Many budget hotels are located on major transport routes such as motorways and near airports, but recently there has been an increase in budget hotels in city centre locations, such as 'Travel Lodge', which has expanded its portfolio in many UK city centre locations.</td></tr>
<tr><td>Size and scale of the sector</td><td>Major operators of budget hotels in UK (2000)
<table>
<tr><th>Brand</th><th>Hotel group</th><th>Number of budget hotels</th></tr>
<tr><td>Travel Lodge</td><td>Forte</td><td>92</td></tr>
<tr><td>Travel Inn</td><td>Whitbread</td><td>59</td></tr>
<tr><td>Granada Lodge</td><td>Granada Group</td><td>21</td></tr>
<tr><td>Campanile</td><td>Societe de Louvre</td><td>15</td></tr>
<tr><td>Premier Lodge</td><td>Greenalls Group</td><td>23</td></tr>
<tr><td>Garden Court</td><td>Holiday Inn</td><td>5</td></tr>
<tr><td>Courtyard</td><td>Marriott</td><td>4</td></tr>
<tr><td>StopInns</td><td>Friendly Hotels</td><td>5</td></tr>
<tr><td>Formule 1</td><td>Accor</td><td>3</td></tr>
<tr><td>Sleep Inn</td><td>Choice 1</td><td>1</td></tr>
</table></td></tr>
<tr><td>Markets served</td><td><ul><li>Business travellers</li><li>Transient UK leisure users – particularly families</li><li>Overseas leisure users – familiar with budget brands, eg French</li><li>First-time/new users attracted by value-for-money (VFM)</li></ul></td></tr>
<tr><td>Product offering</td><td>Rooms are generally equipped with standard 'en-suite' bathroom, telephone, television, but in these establishments many facilities of traditional hotels are not offered, including: porterage, bar, refreshment and breakfast, room service, conference and banqueting and reception seating (based on AA 2 star ratings).

Some budget hotels work in collaboration with local restaurants for food and beverage. This can either be promotion for consumers wishing to dine out or advertised on in-room literature for delivery to substitute for room service. This promotes goodwill and links back to CSR.

Some hotels in this group do not even offer checking-in services: Formule 1 (Accor), has an automated entry service, where the guest swipes their credit card to gain access and the amount is deducted from their account on departure.</td></tr>
<tr><td>Organisation</td><td>Staffing is very limited, possibly just a couple who live on-site and run all operations, with cleaning contracted-out. In essence, budget hotels do not focus on customer service, and guest-staff interaction is very limited.</td></tr>
<tr><td>Current issues and future trends</td><td>Growth in this sector has developed rapidly in recent years, and is expected to rise. 'In 2008, Travelodge unveiled an aggressive expansion strategy to open 44 new hotels across the UK' (www.caterersearch.com). In particular, due to the financial crisis and the impacts on 'discretionary income', the expansion of this type of hotel is likely to increase in the near future.</td></tr>
</table>

A motel that is a hotel located close to a motorway used by drivers to rest between destinations, would, in most cases, be of the same standard as a budget hotel.

Boutique hotels

Factors	Description
Hotel development and location	These days travellers are looking for more than comfort and convenience when it comes to accommodation and with the dominance of the branded hotel chains, discerning customers are looking for products (accommodation) that are less standardised. Conceived in the early 1980s, 'boutique hotels' are more fashionable – *'those who do not stay in boutique hotels are categorised as unfashionable and un-hip' (Anhar* (2001)). In addition, *Hakan et al.* (2006:286) explains: *'Boutique hotels differentiate themselves from larger chain/branded hotels and motels by providing personalised accommodation and services/facilities. Typically, boutique hotels are furnished in a stylish, sometimes themed manner. With 3–100 rooms, most of them are smaller than mainstream hotels, but they are usually equipped with telephone and wireless Internet, air conditioning, mini bars, and cable/ pay TV. Guests are attended to by 24-hour hotel staff. Many boutique hotels have on-site dining facilities, and the majority offer bars and lounges which may also be open to the general public.'* Two of the first boutique hotels in the world were The Blakes Hotel in South Kensington, London (designed by celebrity stylist Anouska Hempel) and the Bedford in Union Square, San Francisco (the first in a series of 34 boutique hotels currently operated under the flag of one of the most eminent players in the boutique hotel world today, the Kimpton Group). In 1984, Ian Schrager opened his first boutique hotel in Murray Hill in New York City: the Morgans Hotel, designed by French stylist Andrée Putnam. Mainly found in lively city destinations, good locations for boutique hotels are not determined only by manner of convenience, but also by the 'trendiness' and 'chic-ness' of their respective neighbourhoods.
Markets served	Boutique hotels generally target customers who are in their early 20s to mid-50s, with mid- to upper-income averages.
Product offering	Boutique hotels are different from traditional hotels for the following reasons: ▪ **Architecture and design:** Style, distinction, warmth, and intimacy are key words in the architecture and design of boutique hotels, Many boutique hotels introduce different themes in each guestroom, making every single stay unique, even for their repeat guests. For example, the Library Hotel in New York City offers a different theme (from romance to music) in every guestroom. ▪ **Service** is enhanced through the connection that hotel guests experience with members of the hotel staff, guests will be addressed to by name by all hotel staff. ▪ **Technology** is used both to create ambience and enhance emotional contact between the guests and the building (such as lighting and music). Technology is also provided for the convenience of hotel guests (in-room DVD players, flat-screen television sets, cordless phones, and computers with high-speed Internet access and the latest monitor genres). ▪ **Entertainment** – in boutique hotels it is important to create a lively, chic and trendy mind-set. Entertainment includes events such as live music and performances; a hip restaurant, lounge, and bar; an exceptional theme; and visually spectacular decorations.

Factors	Description
Current issues and future trends	Once established, boutique hotels tend to have a higher than average percentage of repeat business compared to the industry in general because of their nature and because the customers of boutique hotels are less likely to be affected by difficult economic times. Nevertheless, smart boutique hotels must strive to adapt to incessantly changing needs, tastes, preferences and fashions in order to remain competitive within their niche market.

2.2.2 Guest houses

DEFINITION

'An establishment, licensed or unlicensed, which provides accommodation, meals and sometimes other services for residents only'. (English Tourist Board, ETB)

Generally, guest houses provide accommodation for more than six paying guests, with the owner and staff providing more services, for example, dinner, in the U.K. '*around 70% have less than 25 rooms*' (*Morrison, ibid Jones* (1996: 73)).

Guesthouses are essentially people's homes which have been extended and adapted to accommodate paying guests, and are a significant feature in many seaside towns throughout the UK.

The product generally consists of the following characteristics:

- A warm welcome
- Comfortable facilities
- Attractive location
- Satisfaction of perceptions of 'value for money' (VFM)
- Pride in preparing and serving good-quality local produce
- 'Caring' represented by the owner taking a personal interest in guests
- Tailoring customer service to each individual guest's needs (personal touch)

Morrison, ibid Jones (1996:80)

Current issues and future trends

This sub-sector of the accommodation industry has suffered significantly over the past couple of decades for a number of reasons:

- The increase in cheaper 'package, mass tourism holidays' to sunnier countries in the Mediterranean, such as Spain, Greece and Turkey.
- The increase in budget hotels, offering a better standard of accommodation at a more reasonable price.
- The old-fashioned product of the guest houses, with many not adapting and up-dating their product to meet the needs of younger segments of the market.
- The image of a guesthouse, is perceived as 'old-fashioned' and only for older tourists.

2.2.3 Bed and breakfasts (B&Bs)

Factors	Description
Development and location	Bed and breakfasts are an English phenomenon and can be defined as 'a renovated home, mansion or small hotel – to spend the night and enjoy a full breakfast (included in the price of the room) in the morning' (www.about.com). Bed and breakfasts can be found in most countries, in many locations; city or rural, but the traditional B&B is very common in many of the UK seaside resorts such as Brighton. *'There are an estimated 11,500 B&B's in the UK'* (*Holloway*, 2006:293).

Factors	Description
Markets served	B&Bs' market covers many types of consumers, from those of higher socio-economic groups, who perhaps need to escape the city and require accommodation in a rural setting for a weekend break, or those from lower groups who may see it as a cheap '*informal and friendly*' (*Holloway*, 2006) place to spend their holidays by the sea.
Product offering	The product on offer is relatively simple: guests are provided with a comfortable room, sometimes with a sink, but the bathrooms may be communal and shared with other guests. B&Bs have a very personal approach to guests, similar to guesthouses and the breakfast, normally a traditional 'English breakfast', is served in a small dining area within the establishment.
Current issues and future trends	Many B&Bs in seaside resorts have gone out of business in recent years, particularly due to the increase of cheap foreign holidays to countries such as Spain and Greece. However many still flourish in rural locations, as the need for city dwellers to escape the city has increased increasing the demand for more frequent, shorter breaks. Further, with the weakening pound sterling (£) and the rise of the 'staycation' many people may be attracted to holiday domestically, an advantage for the traditional British B&B.

2.2.4 Farmhouses

Factors	Description
Development and Location	This type of accommodation has grown in recent years, again with the urbanites' need to escape the city plus the supply of rural accommodation from farmers, many of whom have diversified into leisure and tourism, because of the pressures of traditional farming.
Markets served	Farmhouses tend to attract families, especially those with young children and living in cities, seeking a new experience.
Product Offering	Farmhouses, are very similar to rural B&Bs, in that they offer relatively basic accommodation, but in a friendly and comfortable dwelling. A comfortable room is provided and a 'true, hearty' breakfast of locally produced goods. Many farms offer holidays that include working on the farm, and this enables guests to get up close to animals and experience life as a farmer.
Current issues and future trends	'Agri-tourism' has grown in recent years in many countries, as the 'need to escape' has increased, and this trend looks set to develop in the near future, particularly with recession and the rise of the 'staycation'. Recent events, such as the e-coli problems in UK petting farms could have a negative impact on this form of rural tourism.

2.2.5 Self-catered (non-serviced)

Type	Description
Apartments and villas	These are privately-owned by individuals or companies, where the guests provide their own food and do their own cooking. ▪ **Apartments**: are generally found in main tourist centres, particularly in large blocks. These are normally 'self-contained' and offer communal facilities such as swimming pools, tennis courts and shops and restaurants for guests. ▪ **Villas**: large residences in rural or near tourist centres. They can provide accommodation for families with children, or for a couple of families, depending on the size of the property. Some villas may have their own pools, but the main tourist centres and beaches, may be a drive from the property. ▪ **Gites/cottages**: these are generally found in rural locations, and offer accommodation for those who want a peaceful holiday in the countryside. Gites (France) and cottages, are normally older buildings that have been converted for modern living and can accommodate large families or a couple of families. ▪ **ApartHotels:** A relatively new trend. Aparthotels are sometimes are part of the hotel but on occasions, they may be the full hotel. The target customer is long-stay customers. Rooms are specialised as they feature dining area, refrigerator, a small equipped kitchen, microwave and washing machine. Benefits for customers is they have the option of self-catering which reduces the costs associated with hotel dining and laundry.
Campus accommodation	These are university halls of residence, where tourists can rent room out of term time. The accommodation generally consists of a room, with the bathrooms and kitchens to share with other guests. This is a good option for lone travellers, especially younger people, who want clean accommodation for a short period of time, in an urban centre.
Youth hostel	A very popular form of accommodation for younger persons and single travellers. This type of accommodation offers basic facilities and can include a bed in a room with others – 'dormitory'. Youth hostels vary in location from beautiful rural manor houses to city centre blocks, and in the UK the Youth Hostel Association (YHA) runs '*226 youth hostels*' (*Dale*, 2005:16) in varying locations.
Campsites	Privately-owned land, where tourists pay a nightly-fee to pitch their tent or caravan, with washing and electricity sometimes provided. Camping and caravanning holidays have grown substantially in recent years and caravanning alone accounts for '*17% of UK holiday spending*' (*Page & Connell*, 2006:218).

Marriott
EXECUTIVE APARTMENTS
SATHORN VISTA – BANGKOK

FOR DISCUSSION

Have you ever been on a self-catering holiday?

Where did you go?

Who did you go with?

What do you think are the advantages of going on a 'self-catering' holiday?

3 Distribution systems

Distribution systems are the methods used for accommodation operators to **reach** and secure customers. This is not to be confused with advertising. Distribution systems are channels where consumers can **purchase** the product directly or indirectly

> *'A set of interdependent organisations (intermediaries) involved in the process of making a product or service available for use or consumption by the consumer or business user'.*
>
> *Kotler et al.* (2003)

Examples of distribution intermediaries

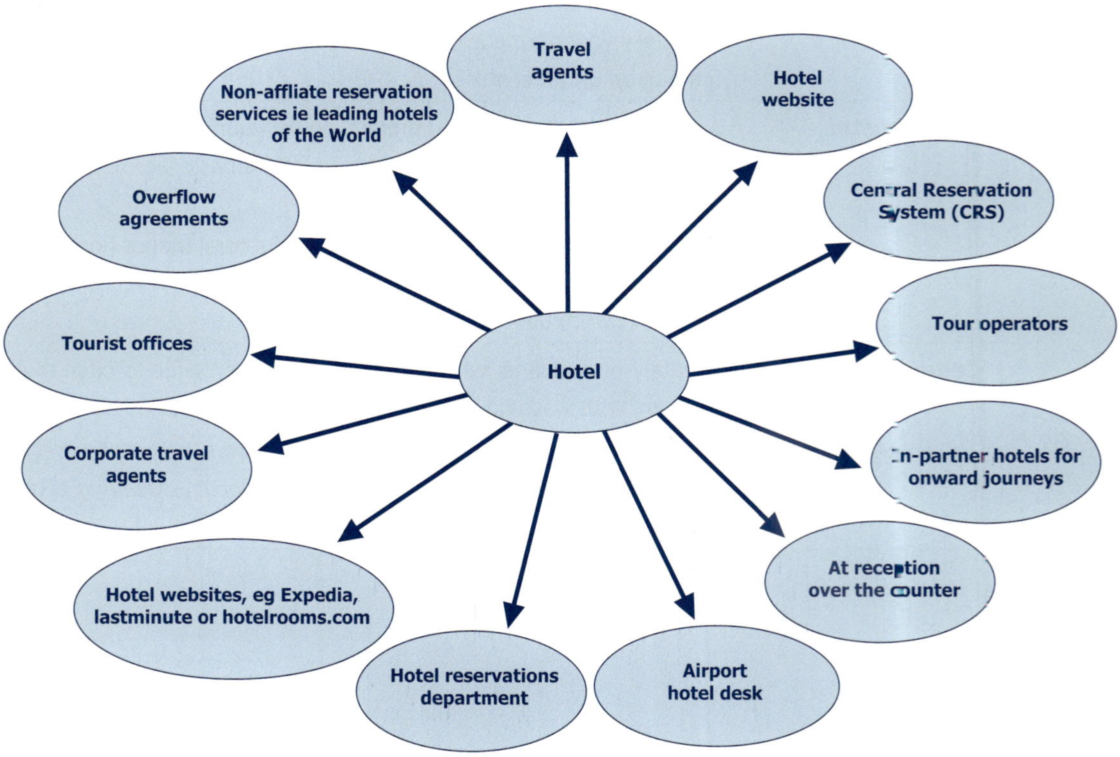

Figure 5.3 Examples of distributions intermediaries

Each type of accommodation presented in this chapter uses different methods of distribution to suit their operation, budget and target market. Furthermore, different hotels will receive varying quantities of bookings from different channels; for example, a 4-star hotel would get a higher percentage of bookings from corporate travel agents than a budget hotel.

Gee (1994): *'an important element in the marketing strategy of any hotel is the system of marketing channels through which products and services are sold to their ultimate buyers'.*

Advantages of distribution channels	Disadvantages
▪ More effective demand management for perishable products	▪ The loss of margin paid to agents through commission
▪ Convenient global/local access points for customers away from the hospitality location	▪ The loss of margin caused by charging tour operators low accommodation rates for volume business
▪ The provision of relevant information and guidance to potential customers by knowledgeable travel experts	▪ Intermediaries can be closer to the end-user, taking ownership of the customer away from the hospitality organisation
▪ The opportunity to work with specialist intermediaries who understand the dynamics of their own markets	

ACTIVITY 2 — 20 minutes

Looking at the below types of consumer depicted below. Which methods do you think they use when booking a hotel room and why?

1

2

3

4

DEFINITION

Global Distribution Systems (GDS)

Kasavana & Cahill (1997) explain that **Global Distribution Systems** *'are often formed as joint ventures linking a number of diverse businesses. By directly linking the reservation system of hotel, airline car rental, and travel agency companies on a worldwide basis through the Internet or private networks, Global Distribution Systems provide access to travel and tourism inventories around the world'.*

- Owned by airlines
- Used by travel agents
- Access travel/tourism inventories worldwide
- Link to reservation systems of:
  - Hotels
  - Airlines
  - Car rental companies

Central Reservations Systems (CRS)

Used by large chains or consortia whereby an off-site facility manned by a team of qualified sales agents is used to receive customers' bookings.

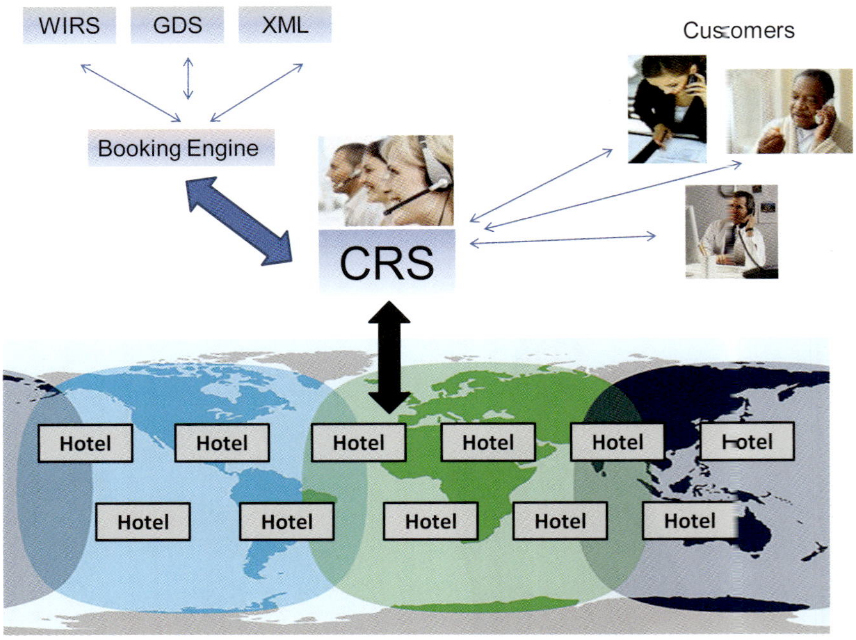

Agents have up-to-date information to hand to assist callers with hotel details	**Maintains statistical information (call volume, talk time, conversion rates, denial rates)**	**Delivers reservations to properties**	**Provide properties with necessary technology**
Agents are sales-orientates	**Communicated room availability to e-distribution channels**	**Provide customer relationship management (loyalty programmes)**	**In most cases CRS offers a toll free number or 0800 number**
Bills properties for reservations handling	**Maintain demographic information about callers**	**CRS offers are off-site allowing for cost savings**	**Sales agents are in most cases multi-lingual**

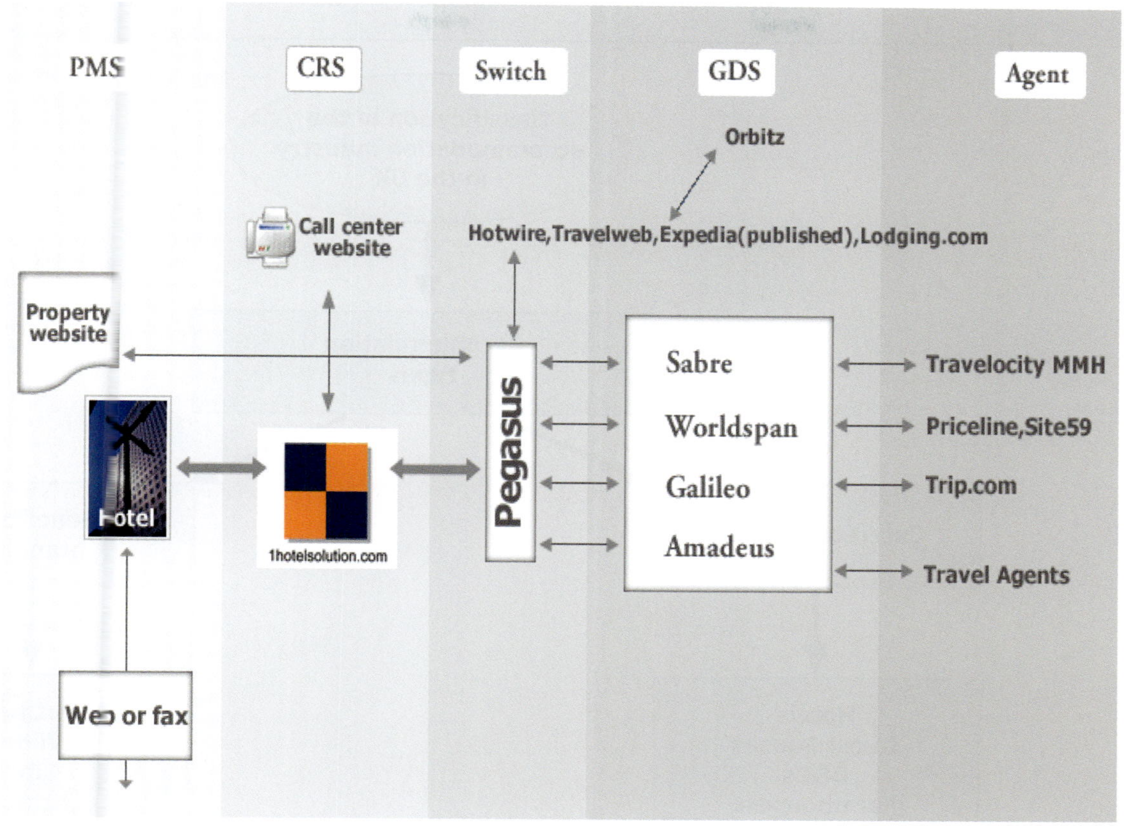

Figure 5.4 Central Reservations Systems

FOR DISCUSSION

Looking at the different forms of 'serviced/catered' accommodation, think of examples of these where you live. Which are the most common? Why do you think these are the most common? Those which you don't have, why do you think there are none where you live?

CHAPTER SUMMARY

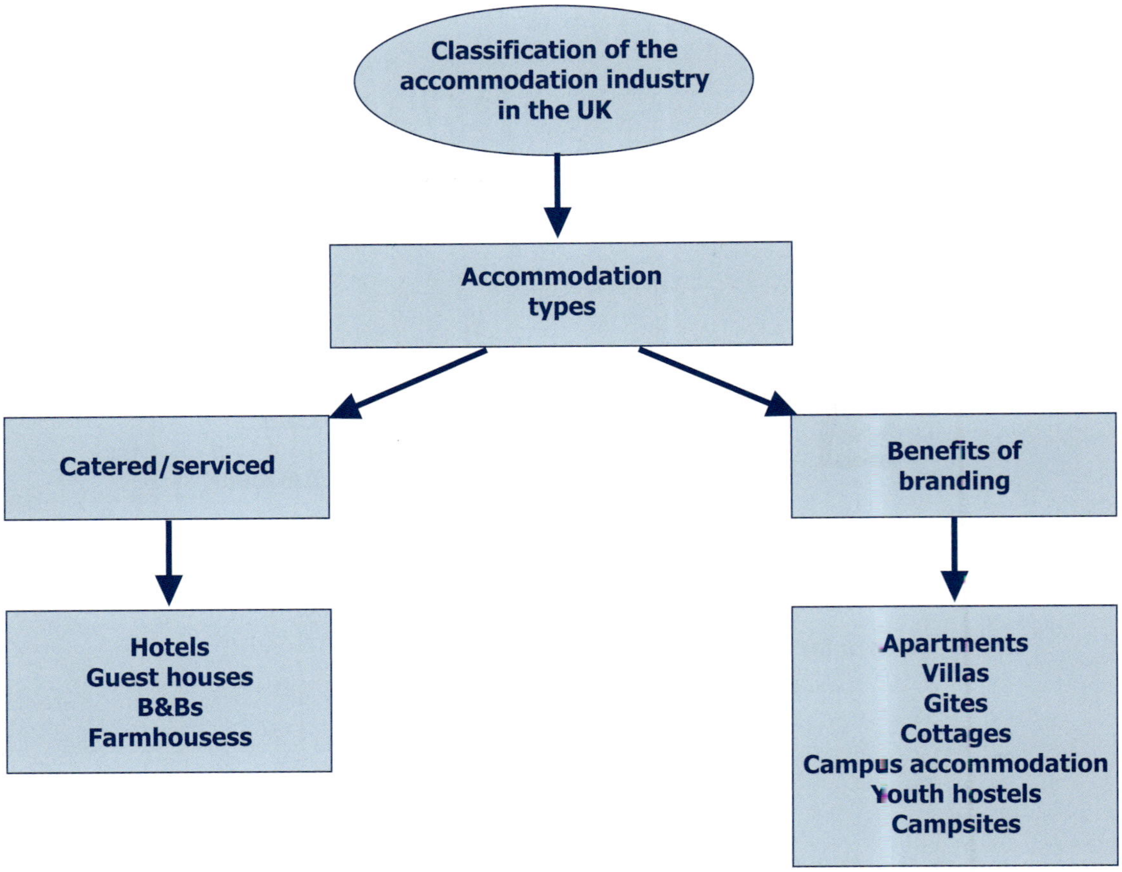

SELF-TEST QUESTIONS

1. Name the two accommodation types.
2. Give a definition of catered accommodation.
3. List the different 'catered' accommodation types.
4. What is 'self-catered' accommodation?
5. List *Jones'* (2002) different sources for demand of accommodation.
6. Looking at Figure 5.1 (Accommodation types), which type of accommodation is most suitable for business travellers?
7. Give a definition of a 'resort hotel'.
8. List the different types of 'self-catered' accommodation.

SELF-TEST ANSWERS

1 The two types of accommodation are: catered (serviced) and self-catered (non-serviced).

2 Catered accommodation normally includes the provision of food for its guests. This can include: breakfast, lunch and an evening meal. Breakfast and an evening meal are classed as 'half board', breakfast, lunch and evening meal is termed 'full-board'.

3 Catered accommodation includes: hotels, guesthouses, bed and breakfasts and farmhouses.

4 Self-catered accommodation provides accommodation with cooking facilities but no food. It is up to the guests to cook or make their own eating arrangements.

5 *Jones'* (2002) different sources for demand of accommodation are:

- Government officials
- Business travellers
- Leisure travellers
- Tour groups
- Conference participants
- Other users

6 The type of accommodation most suitable for business travellers is: airport hotels.

7 A resort hotel is '*the provision of accommodation and substantial other services at one location*' which are '*completely self-contained*', and are generally an all-inclusive package holiday.

8 Motels, inns, state-run establishments, urban hotels' executive residences, apartment hotels (aparthotel) and university accommodation.

ANSWERS TO ACTIVITIES

1 The types of accommodation that are for both business and leisure tourists include:

Airport hotels, motels, inns, state-run establishments, urban hotels, executive residences, university accommodation and apartment hotels.

For leisure tourists only: youth accommodation, cruiseliner, orient express, farm stays, timeshare, caravans/camping, villas, forest villages.

2

1. Businessman – This consumer would most likely book rooms through a corporate travel agent (through his company) and through the Central Reservations System. Being busy he would not have time to use websites and visit travel agents.
2. Young travellers – Probably looking for a deal so would use web portals, for example Travelocity or lastminute.com.
3. Retired couple – Less likely to use the Internet due to unfamiliarity. Travel agents offer security and someone to talk to about the trip, which may be more reassuring.
4. Family – Families tend to have a wide range of needs and therefore contacting a travel agent may be easier than looking for answers online. A central reservations service may also be used.

The above are generalisations and may vary depending on the type of consumer.

CHAPTER 6

THE FOOD SERVICE INDUSTRY

Chapter objectives

In this chapter you will:

- Investigate the motivations for eating out
- Identify the factors in the meal experience
- Be introduced to The UK hospitality 'Standard Industrial Classification' (SIC)
- Understand the different sectors of the food service industry
- Investigate the different types of food service
- Detail and appraise the different food service and production methods
- Investigate legislation in the industry and licensing
- Discuss trends within the food service sector

Topic list

1 The food service industry

Food service has developed into a huge industry. The number and type of eating-out establishments has increased tremendously, as suppliers constantly try to satisfy the changing demands and tastes of the market. In the UK alone there are approximately 300,000 catering outlets, contributing £43 billion to the UK economy (*Foskett et al.*, 2008). Most towns and cities across the world offer a variety of eating establishments with different themes and dishes, to satisfy the needs of an increasingly knowledgeable and demanding population.

Source: Radisson.com

Size and structure of the food and beverage industry

Sector	Outlets	Million meals
Restaurants	26,629	750
Quick Service Restaurants	29,784	2,034
Pubs	50,989	1,125
Hotels	46,562	645
Leisure	19,234	537
Staff Catering	20,436	1,061
Health Care	31,577	1,050
Education	34,608	1,230
Services	3,068	249
Total 2006	262,888	8,682

Source: Horizons Foodservice Intelligence (2006)

Figure 6.1: The United Kingdom Food Service Industry 2006

	1996	1999	2000	%
Restaurants	609	660	676	8
Quick service	1,930	1,908	2,007	23
Pubs	1,036	1,139	1,095	13
Hotels	628	671	677	8
Leisure	506	542	541	6
Staff catering	988	1,032	1,049	13
Healthcare	1,087	1,070	1,086	13
Education	1,274	1,204	1,211	14
Services	233	225	227	2
Total	8,291	8,452	8,569	

Source: Foodservice Intelligence

Figure 6.2: Number of meals served (m), 1996 and 1999–2000

ACTIVITY 1 **15 minutes**

Looking at Figure 6.2:

- What is the most popular type of eating outlet in the UK in 2000?
- What is the least popular type of eating outlet in the UK in 2000?

Have any eating outlets become more popular from 1996–2000?

Have any eating outlets become less popular from 1996–2000?

2 Who eats out and why?

Smith (1967) identified 43 different reasons why people eat out, but he stated six basic reasons why people eat away from their homes.

Reason for eating out	Description
Convenience	People who are away from home fro work or leisure, where it is physically impossible to return home to eat, need to eat close to where they are at that moment in time. Examples may include: fast-food restaurants and sandwich shops.
Variety	People are now more educated about eating, are increasingly adventurous in wanting to sample the food of other cultures. There is also more awareness of food and its connection with health.
Labour	Sometimes people do not have the time or wish to spend it preparing a meal, and then have to clean and wash-up afterwards. Going out to eat takes away all the time and effort.
Status	People may go to eat out to impress other people. An expensive meal or trendy restaurant is a good setting for an important business negotiation.
Culture/tradition	Special events, such as birthdays and religious festivals, can be celebrated by going to a restaurant. In the UK many young Muslims celebrate Eid by going out for a meal.
Impulse	Some people eat out, on the 'spur of the moment'. Possibly prompted by a bad day at work, some good news, they may pass an inviting restaurant and change their dinner plans.

FOR DISCUSSION

When did you last eat out? Where did you eat? What did you eat? Why did you dine out?

2.1 Factors in the meal experience

Factor	Description
Food	**Appearance**: does it look good? '*Looks good enough to eat*'. **Aroma**: does it smell good? Some establishments design ventilation systems giving out smells of the food, so they attract customers in to their outlets. **Taste**: if it does not taste good, people will complain or they will not return.
Service	Customer service is very important and has improved substantially in recent years. Good customer service, recognised by responsiveness to requests, efficient service, accurate bills and the right level of attentiveness, affects the 'dining-out' experience, and results in returning customers and a good ambience. Customer service levels vary depending on the type of establishment. 'High class' restaurants have very personal and high levels of customer service, whereas a 'fast-food' restaurant may have a very impersonal service but effect it just as well.
Cleanliness and hygiene	High standards of cleanliness and hygiene are paramount for a dining outlet. Unhygienic, dirty establishments can make customers ill. A loss of reputation, legal action, and closure often follows. There are three areas of concern: ▪ **Staff** – staff should look clean smart and tidy; some establishments provide a uniform for staff. Furthermore, clean nails, tidy hair and evidence of good hygiene are reassuring for customers. ▪ **Equipment** – must be clean. If it isn't, this can lead to illnesses among staff and customers. Furthermore it can also ensure that machines do not break down. ▪ **Environment** – the restaurant should be immaculate with clean floors, surfaces, toilets, etc. This is part of the experience. No standard of décor can compensate for poorly kept premises.
Décor	The design of the restaurant can add value to the dining experience. Nice paintings, appropriate colours and furnishings, must be suitable for the type of restaurant, or customers may feel uncomfortable. Décor also helps attract passing trade.
Lighting	Lighting creates ambience and again must be appropriate for the style. A fast food shop may have very bright lights (expecting a fast turnover of customers), whereas a traditional restaurant may have more subtle lighting, creating a relaxing atmosphere.
Air-conditioning	This is a necessity in very hot countries, as feeling hot while dining can be a very uncomfortable experience.
Furnishing	Furniture must be suitable for the type and theme of the restaurant. Plastic chairs may be appropriate for a 'fast food restaurant, but are not in a 'high class' restaurant, where the experience should be a relaxing and comfortable one.
Acoustics	▪ **Voices** – it is important to be able to hold a conversation with other diners and with the waiter. ▪ **Music** – can enhance the enjoyment, and appropriate music for the type and theme of restaurant is vital. Furthermore, if the music is too loud, it may spoil the dining experience and prevent repeat business.

Factor	Description
Room proportion	If a room is too big it can feel impersonal, a smaller room can provide intimacy. However, the spacing between tables can make the difference.
Price	Price must be proportionate to the food and service. Better quality ingredients, more qualified chefs and alternative service command higher premiums.
Clientele	Customers' behaviours affect other customers. People talking loudly or singing can ruin the atmosphere. Certain types of restaurants target particular types of customers; McDonald's attract families with young children therefore no one is likely to be upset if there are young children there behaving noisily.

3 Standard Industrial Classification (SIC)

3.1 The UK hospitality 'Standard Industrial Classification' (SIC)

You were first introduced to this classification in Chapter 1.

Division 6		Services	
Class	**Group**	**Activity**	
66			Hotels and Catering
	661		Restaurants, snack bars, cafes and other eating places
		6611	Eating places supplying food for consumption on the premises: (a) licensed (b) unlicensed
		6612	Take-away food shops
	662	6620	Public houses and bars
	663	6630	Nightclubs and licensed clubs
	664	6640	Canteens and messes (a) catering contractors (b) other canteens

3.2 The catering industry 'Standard Industrial Classification' (SIC)

Sector	SIC classification	Differentiating factor
Restaurants	6111	'quintessential food service outlet'
Hotel foodservice	6650	'for people staying away from home'
Motorway and roadside	6611	'foodservice for the motorist'
Licensed trade	6620 and 6630	'food for people out for a drink'
Fast food and take aways	6612 and 6611	'meal package for people in a hurry'
Employee-feeding	6640	'for people at their workplace'
Welfare catering	9310, 9320 and 9330	'for people unable to feed themselves'
Travel catering		'for people on the move'
Outside and social catering		'service where it was never intended'

Jones (1997:117)

3.3 Types of foodservice or catering

Foodservice is a large industry and is found in many types of operations as detailed below.

Shopping malls, airports, food courts	**Ethnic restaurants (Chinese, Japanese, French, Malaysian, Caribbean)**	**Ethnic chains (Wagamama, Bombay Bicycle, Yo Sushi, Nandos)**	**Educational institutions (schools, colleges, universities)**
Transport (rail, air and marine)	**Welfare catering (hospitals, healthcare, prisons, military)**	**Restaurants (bistros, brasseries, coffee shops, cafeterias, wine bars, public houses, roadside restaurants)**	**Supermarkets – food retail (food to go)**
Employee dining	**Outside catering**	**Private clubs**	**Street vendors**
Fine dining	**Themed restaurants (Hard Rock Café, Planet Hollywood)**	**Cafés and sandwich bars**	**Fast food chains (McDonald's, Subway, KFC, Wendy's)**
Accomodation (hotels, motels, guest houses, hostels)	**Leisure (museums, theme parks, theatres, cinemas)**	**Conference centres**	**Take-away (kiosks, fish and chips, snack bars)**

Catering type	Description
Restaurant	The restaurant industry is made of many different themed speciality restaurants. They may vary as well in the type of service they offer: fast food or gourmet dining. They are priced accordingly – with quick service restaurants offering a low price, mid-scale offering 'value and comfort' and 'upscale outlets' offering 'experience, style and ambience' at a high price. (see Section 4.1)
Hotel foodservice	See Figure 6.3 below
Motorway and roadside	These establishments can be found 'out-of-town', on motorways and roadside, and generally provide a mix of catering outlets selling meals, snacks and refreshments for people travelling by car, coach or lorry.
Licensed trade (public houses – 'pubs')	Many establishments licensed for the 'sale of drinks for consumption generally on the premises', such as: bars, clubs and pubs, have in recent years begun to offer catering in the form of snacks, such as sandwiches and bar meals. Many larger establishments, such as chain pubs, have a separate dining area where a full menu is on offer including starters, main courses and desserts.
Fast food and take-aways	Fast food and take-aways serve *'people in a hurry'*. World-wide the industry is huge. In the United States alone, industry sales were worth around US$142 billion (2006: The National Restaurant Association).

Catering type	Description
Employee feeding	Ancillary facilities can be seen as a benefit or 'perk', and regarded as a differentiating factor among companies wishing to attract good calibre staff. Employee feeding, whether by 'self-operated facilities' or 'contracted services' can take different forms depending on the size and type of organisation. These include: ▪ **Automatic vending** – vending machines selling hot and cold drinks, confectionery and snacks, sandwiches and meals (hot and cold). ▪ **Trolley service** – 'tea-trolleys', once a very popular service, delivering mid-morning or afternoon tea and coffee to employees at their workplace or station. ▪ **Cafeteria** – 'In-line/straight-line', a single counter where food is displayed from starter through to dessert and drinks, and customers push their trays to the till at the end of the counter. 'Free-flow' – different counters offering different food items. 'Carousel' – rotating shelves where customers help themselves to food offerings.
Welfare catering	'The provision of meals for those unable to feed themselves' (*Brotherton*, 2003) and generally includes foodservice in education, healthcare and social care and prisons.
Travel catering	Catering which can be found on aircraft, ships and trains.
Outside and social catering	Catering provided at events such as fetes and exhibitions can be divided into two types: Contracted and Speculative functions. ▪ **Contracted**: catering provided for a specified and agreed number of customers. ▪ **Speculative**: contracted to provide refreshment on a site for people attending a particular event, such as a sporting event, for example, The Wimbledon Tennis Championships or Grand Prix motor racing.

Hotel food service		Availability	Menus
Coffee shop	The coffee shop is normally one of the largest outlets in the hotel. Busiest: breakfast, evenings and weekends. Food offered tends to be a mix of local and international dishes. Customers tend be a mix of in-house residents and locals.	Open from breakfast through to dinner. Some hotels offer a 24 hour coffee shop.	Buffet: breakfast, lunch and dinner. Basic *À la carte* menu throughout the day. Lunch and dinner *table d'hôte* (set menu).
Restaurant	Most 4- or 5-star hotels normally feature a specialist restaurant offering a specific theme or concept. Busiest: evenings, weekends and special occasions (ie Valentines and holidays). Food offered could be Chinese, Japanese, Middle Eastern or any other international theme or concept. Customers tend be a mix of in-house and local residents.	Lunch and dinner.	*À la carte* Wine list

Hotel food service		Availability	Menus
Fine dining	Some hotels feature a fine dining restaurant. Very high quality food, beverages and service in a comfortable and professional environment.	Mostly evening service only (some lunchtimes).	*À la carte* Wine and drinks list Cigar list Liqueur trolley
Bar	Hotel bars are sometimes attached to hotel coffee shops or can be independent and in a different location within the hotel. Busiest: lunchtimes, evenings and on weekends. Some bars offer live music and feature television sports, which can attract customers. Customers tend be a mix of in-house residents and locals.	Midday to late.	Bar snack menu Drinks list Cigar list
Lounge	Most hotels normally offer a lounge seating area either close to reception or in another part of the hotel.	Throughout the day.	Hot and cold beverages Snack menu Afternoon tea or desserts
Executive lounge	Nowadays, most 4- and 5-star hotels feature an executive lounge to accommodate business guests exclusively.	Throughout the day.	Complimentary beverages, evening snacks and *à la carte* breakfast.
Conference and Banqueting	The Conference and Banqueting facilities normally comprise of rooms of different sizes to accommodate varying types of events and numbers. Some hotels may just have a few small meeting rooms, while others may have large scale ballrooms. Busiest: Religious holidays, wedding and conference season. Customers tend be a mix of in-house residents and locals.	When booked.	Delegate meal packages Banquet menus Wine and drinks list
Outside catering	When a hotel or food and beverage operation produces and/or delivers food and beverage to an event/service outside the normal premises.	When booked.	Conference and Banqueting or bespoke menu.
Room service	Room service is the delivery of food and beverages to customers in their hotel room. Room service also has the responsibility of pre-delivering complimentary food and beverage amenities to the room, such as chocolates, fruit baskets and champagne.	24 hours.	Room service *À la carte* menu

Hotel food service		Availability	Menus
Mini bar	Mini bars are located in the hotel room and feature a combination of cold snacks, alcoholic and non-alcoholic beverages. Mini bars are maintained by either room service or a mini bar attendant. Customers pay on departure.		Mini bar menu
Guest amenities	Complimentary food and beverage delivered to the room. Normally organised by guest relations and delivered by the room service department to either a regular, new or dissatisfied guest.		Examples: Champagne, wine, fruit basket, cheese board, dates or chocolates
Employee dining	Hotels normally provide an in-room dining facility for employees free of charge usually. It can be managed either by the Human Resources Department or Food and Beverage. In some situations it can be outsourced.	Breakfast, lunch and dinner. Food themes should reflect the workforce's needs.	Buffet, cafeteria and vending options

Figure 6.3: Hotel food and beverage

4 Restaurants

DEFINITION

Restaurant – *'an establishment where refreshments or meals may be obtained.'* *Jones* (1996:122)

Restaurants can fall into three categories in terms of ownership:

Restaurant type	Description
Independent restaurants	Independent restaurants are owned by individuals, such as a family, and despite the large number of chain restaurants *Jones* (1996) identifies that '*restaurants tend to be owned by individuals and individualists*'.
Chain restaurants	*'One of two or more restaurants normally owned by a company and marketed on a corporate basis.'* *Brotherton* (2003:36) Chain restaurants are normally big brands that have standard menus, design, name, with all the outlets very similar in layout, and design following a particular theme. Chain restaurants are either: ▪ Franchises, where an individual owns the restaurant and pays the 'franchiser' (the big company) to use the fittings, name, menu etc. ▪ Management companies, that is companies that run and own a number of restaurants.

Restaurant type	Description
Franchises	These are generally associated with the big brand names in the catering industry, with many 'fast food' outlets, owned and controlled in this manner. Individuals 'franchisee' may own and run the restaurant, but they pay to use the name etc of the 'franchiser'.

FOR DISCUSSION

Can you think of any examples of: independent restaurants, chain restaurants and franchises in your area?

What types of food do they serve? Who are their customers?

4.1 Types of restaurants

It is not only ownership that can determine the structure of the restaurant industry. *Chon and Sparrowe* (2000), identify the structure of the industry according to concept, menu and market.

- Fine dining restaurants – Personalised service with high standards of product and service
- Theme restaurants – For example – Hard Rock Café, Planet Hollywood
- Ethnic restaurants – Chinese, Indian, Thai, Japanese
- Family restaurants – Pizza Hut, Harvester
- Quick service/fast food restaurants – McDonald's, KFC, Taco Bell
- Grill/buffet

These restaurants can be distinguished by their style and possibly by food type, but price and clientele are also important factors in segmenting the restaurant sector, therefore *Muller and Woods* (1994) identify five segments as listed below.

Restaurant type	Description
Quick-service	A consistent product with fast service at a low price.
Mid-scale	'Family restaurants', comfortable surroundings, value-for-money ('VFM') convenience, large menu including kids menu; with table or counter service. Other services for families may include baby change facilities, high chairs and activities for children.
Moderate upscale	'Casual theme' restaurants, where there is a good atmosphere and flexibility, therefore it is used by many different market sectors.
Upscale	Mainly 'independently-owned', which have higher prices and the focus is the experience: personalised, image, quality, style and atmosphere.
Business dining	'Contract caterers', for business clients, generally focus on: locations (near offices etc), VFM, price and changing menus – to keep customers interested.

4.2 Fast food and take-aways

These types of food outlets are 'for people in a hurry', and the industry globally, is huge, '*in the United States alone, industry sales were worth around US$142 billion in 2006* (The National Restaurant Association). Definitions of the fast food industry are product-based, and generally have four features:

DEFINITION

Perishability – the life of the product is very short, minutes or hours.

Fast product finishing – this means the time from placing the order to the customer consuming the product is very short. It varies depending on the restaurant and type of food ordered, but it should be between two and 15 minutes, if ordered on-site. Some restaurants even promote standards so that if you do not receive your food in a set time, say ten minutes, you can have it free.

Hand/fingers-held product – most fast food can be eaten without cutlery and if necessary on the move, ie while walking.

Low selling price – generally fast food is cheap compared with other types of restaurants.

Source: dietsinreview.com

Very few areas of the globe have successfully resisted the entry of the fast food restaurant into their environment. Franchising has fuelled the growth of these chained fast food outlets.

In a survey conducted by *Walker* (1989), the major benefits perceived by franchisors from international expansion were related to financial, market or general growth.

Benefits by franchisors

- Additional growth/expansion
- Added revenues/profits, improved return on investment, or direct financial gain
- Larger market, more market penetration, increased market share
- International identity, greater recognition

Drawbacks for franchisors

- Lack of control
- Difficulty in supporting franchisees
- Cost/expense involved
- Distance and possible time difference

FOR DISCUSSION

Think of fast-food outlets in your area/city. What types of food do they serve? Who eats in the fast food restaurants? Do they have seating? Where are they located?

Your answers may have identified that fast-food restaurants are often owned by big, heavily branded chains, with the same themes, décor and menus rolled out to all the outlets. Products are limited and priced cheaply.

4.2.1 The main features of the fast food chain restaurant

Tangible elements	
Food and drink	Limited menu, consistent quality, equally portioned, low prices.
Secondary items	Newspapers, children's activities/party-ware.
Physical environment	Clean, bright, modern, carefully laid out.
Packaging	Disposable, easy to handle, maintain temperature of food.

Intangible elements	
Personal contact	Staff-customer contact – technology-led and brief.
Service delivery	Eat on the premises, take-away, 'drive-thru' or delivered to customer.
Promotion	'VFM', emphasis on promoting to children – links with 'kids' films', characters.
Outlet atmosphere	Bright colours, plants, music, corporate identity prominent.
Location	Convenient by foot or car – accessible.
Emotions of customer	Aim to satisfy with offer.
Post-transaction service	Complaints, satisfaction a key feature, especially of the bigger brands.

ACTIVITY 2 **Homework**

Research a 'fast-food' outlet that you know of, it could be a branded chain restaurant or a smaller fast-food outlet.

Research the history of the company, how many outlets it has, how many staff it employs and the food it offers.

5 Contract catering and employee feeding

Contract catering is concerned with catering companies providing food and refreshments for organisations which prefer to 'outsource' their catering operations, such as staff meals.

Non-commercial food service operation normally operates in other facilities where providing food and beverage is not the primary mission.

Characteristics of non-commercial operations

- Non-commercial institutions hire commercial food service management (contract) companies from outside to manage food service in their institutions.
- Commercial food service management companies exist to make profit.
- They carry out fully the food and service responsibilities for the institutions under contract.
- The institution or workplace can free itself from the day-to-day concern of managing food service operations.
- They are professional food service companies.
- These operations are planned to keep the expenses/costs low; they are budget-oriented.
- They are part of properties that exist for reasons other than the service of food and beverage. The service of food and beverage is only supportive.
- Competition is limited as the service is provided in a private, closed environment.

- Normally large scale, delivered at particular times of day.
- Business levels are quite predictable making it easier for production and planning.

The sectors that normally require 'contract catering' include:

- Business and industry
- Education
- The military
- Healthcare
- Prisons
- Transportation

An organisation (client) signs a 'contract' with a catering company for a set period of time, to provide a set number of meals within that organisation. Many different organisations have varying needs for their 'in-house' catering therefore a number of contracts are available:

Contract type	Description
Executive lease	The contract catering company provides an executive who directs the catering operation, overseeing the catering staff, which is provided by the client (in-house). The executive guides and advises the 'in-house' staff in the provision of catering within the company.
Management	The catering firm provides all the catering for the company (client), including 'on-site' staff, but facilities and equipment are provided 'in-house' by the client. An invoice is submitted to the client at the end of each month, detailing the expenditure and income of the operation.
Fixed price	This is a 'set' price, normally for a whole year.
Concession	A contractor takes on a contract to provide the catering in an organisation. The contractor performs all the catering operations, and all the expenditures are the concern of the contractor, and any profits made are retained by the contractor.
Fees	Fees are set in a number of ways: ▪ A set annual figure, on a monthly or weekly basis ▪ A percentage of takings or costs ▪ Per meal charge

FOR DISCUSSION

Why do you think companies 'contract-out' their catering?

What are the advantages of contracting/outsourcing catering?

Are there any disadvantages of outsourcing catering?

5.1 Employee feeding operations

Type of operation	Description
Automatic vending	Vending machines are a very common sight in the modern-day workplace. '*By the 1950s it was clear that the future (of vending) lay in servicing the worker and his refreshment needs*' (*Jones*, 1996:196). There are four main categories: ▪ **Beverages**: drinks hot or cold ▪ **Confectionery and snacks**: branded sweets and chocolate ▪ **Sandwiches**: pre-packed in chilled machines ▪ **Meals**: hot or cold – stored in refrigerated units, with microwaves closely located to heat-up the food.
Trolley service	These were once a very common sight in the workplace, especially in offices and factories. Mid-morning and afternoon refreshments are offered at the employee's work-station, without the need for them to leave their workspace.
Cafeteria operations	Cafeterias (cafés) are relatively common in the workplace, especially in large companies with many employees, such as large office blocks. There are **three main systems**: ▪ '**In-line**' – a single counter, where customers take a tray and choose the food on offer. ▪ '**Free-flow**' – several counters, each offering different items. ▪ '**Carousel**' – large rotating shelves.

FOR DISCUSSION

Do any of these employee feeding operations exist in your workplace or college?

If so, what do they offer/vend?

5.2 Public sector and welfare catering

This type of catering is non-profit for the provider, although a public organisation may sub-contract some parts of the operation to a private for-profit company. Public sector catering generally relates to the provision of food and refreshments in the following.

Sector	Description
Education	Schools, colleges and universities require food for staff and students. Facilities may differ depending on the size and age of the students. Many schools offer hot meals and new regulations set standards of food quality and nutrition: 'the balance of good health', to enable students to eat a well-balanced meal at least once a day. Much larger universities may offer a range of catering facilities, including: snack bars, vending machines, canteens and restaurants, providing a range of options for the diverse student population.
Healthcare	Public (NHS) and private hospitals must provide food to patients of all ages, within strict regulations and dietary requirements.
Social care (welfare catering)	Welfare catering relates to meals for the elderly or infirm in the form of meals on wheels, or in day centres and care homes. Emphasis is placed on nutrition in these types of environment.

Sector	Description
Prisons	Catering in prisons can be provided by contract caterers or the prison service, where prison officers and inmates prepare and cook the food, and enable prisoners to gain catering qualifications. The supplies are either provided by local producers or prison farms and gardens, where fruit and vegetables are grown.

5.3 Travel catering

'Travel-related' catering outlets offer a range of meals, snacks and refreshments 'for people on the move', and are centred around the four main ways of travelling: air, rail, road and sea.

Travel catering	Description
Airline catering	This is concerned with food and refreshments provided on aircraft. The type of food and options available differ considerably, depending on the type of flight: international or domestic; the class of ticket; first class or standard and the type of airline: no-frills, scheduled or charter. For example, a first class ticket includes a wide menu and choice of drinks, whereas a standard ticket offers a menu with fewer choices. Now no-frills budget airlines charge passengers for their food, chosen generally from a very limited menu, on flights of under two hours.
Rail catering	Many large railway stations offer a number of catering outlets, generally in the form of branded, fast food outlets, but catering is still offered on-board, usually of three types: ▪ **Buffet bar**: these offer a range of snacks and beverages, for consumption at your seat. ▪ **Restaurant car**: a carriage that is set-up as a restaurant. They offer a range of meals from a menu, and have a number of seatings, including: breakfast (English or continental), lunch and dinner. Passengers are served at their table by a waiter, as in a traditional restaurant. ▪ **Trolley service**: an 'at-seat' service, that provides cold snacks, such as sandwiches, and hot and cold drinks.
Road	'Roadside catering' generally consists of motorway service areas, which offer a number of different catering outlets, such as fast food, restaurants and snack bars. Other 'roadside catering' operations include: roadside diners and restaurants which are normally found on major 'trunk' roads.
Sea travel	▪ **Short sea routes**: Ferries provide a range of catering facilities for the different type of users of this type of transport. Generally, fast food, restaurants, and snack bars are found on short sea routes ferries. ▪ **Cruise ships**: these floating hotels provide a high standard of food and beverages for the guests. This generally includes three seatings including: breakfast, lunch and dinner, where guests are tended to at their tables by waiters, who are designated a number of tables, providing a high standard level of service, including 'silver service'.

6 Legislation and health and safety

Name	Description
RIDDOR	**Reporting Injuries, Diseases and Dangerous Occurrences** This regulation came into being in 1996, and requires accidents, diseases and dangerous occurrences in businesses to be reported and recorded.
COSHH	**Control of Substances Hazardous to Health** All staff working in the catering industry have to be aware of dangerous substances, which can be found in chemicals. These chemicals which can be found in cleaning products are labelled: very toxic, toxic, irritant or corrosive, and all staff must be aware of the dangers of using these products.
Health and Safety at Work Act (1974)	This Act has two main aims: ▪ To extend the coverage and protection of the law to all employees and employers. ▪ To increase awareness of safety among those at work, both employers and employees.
Food Labelling Regulations (1984/1999)	▪ The name of the food and list of ingredients must appear on the label. ▪ An indication of shelf life or a 'use by' date must be clearly visible. ▪ Any special storage conditions have to be specified. ▪ Conditions of use. ▪ Name and address of the manufacturer, packer or seller.
The Food Safety General Food Hygiene Regulations (1995)	▪ To operate hygienically. ▪ Premises must be kept clean and in good repair. ▪ Food-handlers must be trained in food hygiene matters.
Food Safety Act (1990)	▪ The Food Safety (General Food Hygiene) Regulations (1995) ▪ Food Safety (Temperature Control) Regulations (1995) ▪ The Food Premises (Registration) Regulations (1997)

7 The future of the industry

7.1 Credit crunch

The future of the food service industry was looking positive and the forecasts were that all areas of the sector would grow, due to the demand for convenience foods and relatively prosperous economic activity. But in recent years due to the 'credit crunch' the sector has been hit by economic crisis, customers are seeking value-for-money (VFM) and have reduced disposable income.

This 'credit crunch' has affected catering outlets in the following ways:

- Many restaurants have introduced better special offers
- Competition between eateries has become even more intense
- Customers are looking for better VFM
- Restaurant owners need to find ways in which to supply good value

In order to overcome these negative economic impacts catering outlets have had to cut costs by using online distributors of cheap catering equipment and where possible buying in bulk.

7.2 Environmental issues

In the past decade, respect for the environment has become a big issue. Many organisations have had to change their operations to accommodate environmental concerns and to show their 'green credentials' to consumers.

To be more environmentally conscious, guidelines have been established to make the catering industry more energy efficient and sustainable.

Area guidelines	Description
Staff and public facilities	■ Occupancy detectors for lighting and extractor fans.
Storage	■ Cold room and appliance doors to be closed when they are not in use. ■ When stock is low transfer the contents to other units and switch the empty cabinets or rooms off. (Most modern cabinets only take between one and two hours to reach optimum temperature.)
Preparation	■ Use sensor taps to avoid water wastage.
Cooking	■ Refrigeration to the minimum level. ■ Keep equipment clean as this can have a major impact on its efficiency. As a minimum, equipment should be cleaned after every service. ■ Purchase equipment that has low energy consumption while on standby or idle mode. ■ Try to match the amount of food cooked with the amount consumed as this saves on: transport, raw ingredients, the storage, preparation, cooking and disposal of the food.
Service	■ Use time switches to control display lighting. ■ When units are not being used to display hot or cold food switch them off and use the fluorescent light fittings to create the ambience.
Utensil wash	■ When possible only operate the pot wash machine when you have a full load.
Dining area	■ Use natural ventilation whenever possible to provide comfort cooling. ■ Consider enhancing blinds with thermally lined curtains to reduce heat loss through windows. ■ Arrange furniture so that it does not obstruct radiators. ■ Make the maximum use of natural daylight. (Consider fitting daylight sensors to areas that receive natural light to turn off lighting and maximise the use of daylight.) ■ Use energy efficient light bulbs whenever possible.
Wash-up	■ All commercial dishwashers require water, energy and detergents for them to perform successfully; therefore a machine that makes the most effective use of these elements should be selected. ■ Only use dishwashing and glass washing machines when full.
Waste disposal	■ Reduce the amount of waste generated by encouraging waste minimisation and recycling practices.

Area guidelines	Description
All areas	▪ Raise awareness amongst the staff as to the cost of energy and enlist their support in finding savings. ▪ Regularly look around and identify any equipment that is switched on but is not in use and report those findings back to the staff. ▪ Train staff not to switch equipment on until it is needed and switch it off immediately after use. (Consider putting up signage showing the equipment preheat times in the area concerned.) ▪ Ensure that all equipment is correctly insulated to maintain its correct operating conditions. ▪ Carry-out planned preventative maintenance to ensure that all equipment is working to its maximum efficiency. ▪ Seek to surpass current best practice expectations in reducing carbon emissions by reducing the amount of energy that is consumed and wasted. ▪ Through design and procurement, encourage sustainable buying and consumption patterns.

Source: www.fcsi.org.uk

ACTIVITY 3 **Homework**

Investigate a restaurant in your local area; look at ways it is trying to be 'environmentally-friendly'.

Do they recycle? Do they use recycled products? Do they have signs informing staff and customers to turn off lights...?

Food service methods

Source: Foodandbeverageunderground.com

There are various ways that operators can serve food to customers:

Table service	The customer is served at a laid table. This type of service, which includes plated service or silver service, is found in many types of restaurants, cafés and in banqueting.
Self-service	The customer is required to help themselves from a buffet or counter. This type of service can be found in cafeterias and canteens.
Assisted service	The customer is served part of the meal at the table and is required to obtain part through self-service from some form of display or buffet. This type of service is found in 'carvery' type operations and is often used for meals such as breakfast in hotels. It may also be used for functions.
Single point service	The customer orders, pays and receives the food and beverages, for instance at a counter, at a bar in licensed premises, in a fast food operation or at a vending machine.
Specialised service	The food and drink is taken to where the customer is. This includes tray service in hospitals and aircraft, trolley service, home delivery, lounge and room service.

More specific techniques are detailed below.

Method	Description	Opportunities	Challenges
Plate service	Food is prepared in kitchen and placed on individual plates for delivery by service staff to customers. Uses: Hotel and independent restaurants	Kitchen maintains: ▪ Presentation ▪ Quality ▪ Portion control	▪ Need high quantity and highly skilled chefs ▪ Customers sometimes have to wait for food delivery
Buffet service	Food is prepared in advance in kitchen. Large quantities of food is then placed in containers and served from a table in the restaurant. Customers either help themselves or are assisted by either chefs or service staff. Uses: Conference & Banqueting	▪ Can serve large quantities of people ▪ Customers have choice ▪ Customers are part of the process ▪ Fewer staff required ▪ Service staff require less skills ▪ Few customer complaints due to their decision making	▪ Queuing ▪ 'All you can eat' image ▪ Food presentation can be affected ▪ Food can run out ▪ Food quality can be affected due to changes in temperature and mixing of service cutlery ▪ Foreign bodies in food

Method	Description	Opportunities	Challenges
Family service (English service)	Food is prepared in kitchen and placed in bowls or on. Server then transports to restaurant and it is placed in the centre of tables. Customers then help themselves by serving the food onto their empty plates. Uses: Chinese & Middle Eastern Cultures	▪ Less demands on kitchen ▪ Visual for customers ▪ Customer are in control of quantity and selection ▪ Does not demand highly skilled service staff ▪ Highly convenient for customers	▪ Food temperatures can change ▪ Food distribution can be inconsistent
Silver service (Russian Service)	Food is prepared and cooked in kitchen placed on hot silver platters or containers. Server collects platter using a waiter's cloth and goes to restaurant. Using a large spoon and fork server transfers food onto the customer's plate. Uses: Some fine dining and conference and banqueting	▪ Highly personalised service ▪ Reduces pressure on kitchen	▪ Requires very highly skilled service staff ▪ High labour cost ▪ Kitchen loses control in relation to plate presentation ▪ For customers service can be slow, interruptive and sometimes dangerous ▪ Old fashioned
Gueridon or Flambé service	Food is prepped in kitchen but not cooked. Server puts food on a portable trolley and transfers into front of house area. The trolley is placed next to the customer's table and the waiter prepares or cooks the food in front of the customer. The server then puts the food onto a plate and it is placed in front of the customer. Uses: Fine dining restaurants Examples: Flambéed dishes, filleting fish, carving meats.	▪ Highly personalised service ▪ Visual and aromatic ▪ Waiter becomes the chef and artist ▪ Entertainment for the customer ▪ Customer feels more involved in the process	▪ High labour cost ▪ Not suitable for large numbers

Figure 6.4: Food service techniques

ACTIVITY 4 — 45 minutes

Research the following other types of food service method and appraise their strengths and weaknesses.

	Description	Strengths	Weaknesses
Tray service			
Cafeteria service			
Drive thru			
Vending			
Cocktail			
Home delivery			
Take-away			

Visit some restaurants in your area and identify which service methods are being used.

Food production

Food production is the method chosen by the organisation to produce the food for the customer

Source: http://images.google.co.uk/imgres?imgurl=http://farm4.static.flickr.com

Food production methods

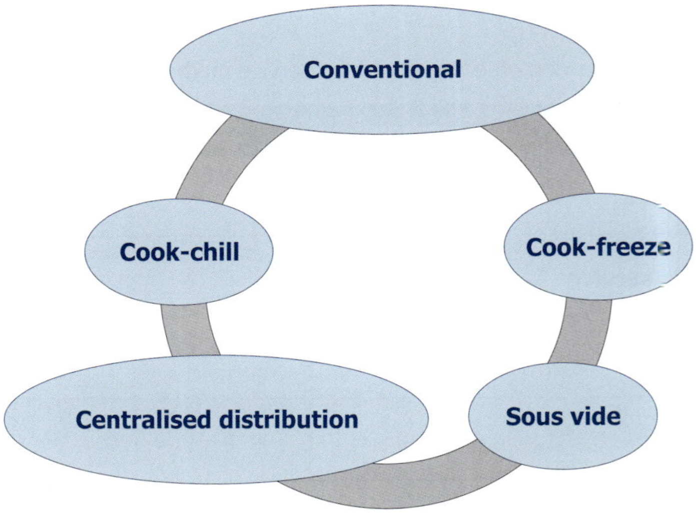

Method	Description
Conventional method	Food is prepared by chefs in the kitchen using traditional techniques such as grilling, steaming, frying and roasting. This method is used in most small independent and high class restaurants.
Centralised	Centralised food production is when the food is produced in bulk off-site. The method is frequently adopted by large chains that are looking to outsource all or part of their food production. Some large chains have their own CPUs while others may use other food production companies.
Sous vide	In the *sous vide* method of food production, foods are prepared and cooked as normal but then portioned into individual plastic bags, chilled and reheated when ordered.
Cook-chill	'Cook-chill is a catering system based on normal preparation and cooking of food followed by rapid chilling storage in controlled low-temperature conditions above freezing point, 0-3°C (32–37°F) and subsequently reheating immediately before consumption. The chilled food is regenerated in finishing kitchens which require low capital investment and minimum staff. Almost any food can be cook chilled provided that the correct methods are used during preparation'. *Source:* Foskett *et al.* (2004)
Cook-freeze	This method is similar to cook-chill apart from the refrigeration temperatures. 'Cook freeze is a specialised food production and distribution system that allows caterers to take advantage of the longer life of blast freezing at 18–20°C (0–32°F) and stored at that temperature until required for resale or consumption for up to three to six months. Blast freezers have increasingly been introduced with success into catering operations. The ability to freeze cooked and prepared dishes, as distinct from storage of chilled foods in a refrigerator or already frozen commodities in a deep freeze allows a caterer to make more productive use of kitchen staff. It also enables economies to be introduced into the staffing of dining rooms and restaurants.' *Source:* Foskett *et al.* (2004)

Trends in food service and production

Trends	
Vegetarianism	Around 5% of the UK population are vegetarian.
Organic food	Consumers increasingly demand food that is healthy, organic and produced without any artificial additives.
Exotic	Consumers increasingly enjoy more exotic foods from areas such as Japan, China, Thailand and India.
Healthier options	Increasing obesity levels are leading consumers to be more health conscious.
Fair trade	The fair treatment of food producers along the food chain with emphasis on fair ethical treatment and payment. Frequently, the fair trade term is visible when producing coffee and fruits from developing economies.
Food miles	The total mileage that food travels from plough to plate. Many foods now available in the West are produced and imported from far distant countries. Although this provides a good range of products accessible all year round certain groups are concerned about the environmental impacts of transporting food long distances. Another consideration is that often the foods being imported are produced locally in the country of importation.
Carbon footprints	The total set of greenhouse gas emissions consumed by the company or product during its production.
Environmental concerns	Food service operators are starting to take a closer look at their energy usage within their operations with reference to the impact on the environment.
Greater transparency	There is a growth in consumers wanting to see greater transparency in relation to knowing where the food served has come from and how it has been produced. Also known as 'Food Provenance' which details information of how the food has travelled from 'farm to fork'.
Outsourcing	The industry is seeing a growing trend in hotels outsourcing their food and beverage to other branded formats. This provides guaranteed monthly rental income for the hotel and provides in-house customers with a more familiar brand. See further details below.
Obesity	The UK is currently experiencing an obesity epidemic and is amongst the most overweight population in Europe. Forecasters predict that more than 12 million adults and one million children will be obese by 2010. A person is classed as obese where their weight has reached a point where it can seriously damage their health. Food service operators are attempting to respond to this issue by offering healthier options on menus.

Outsourcing

Outsourcing is a relatively new trend in food and beverage. More hotels are realising that their own restaurants are unprofitable. The reason for this is that many residents prefer to dine out in food and beverage branded outlets that are known to them. In response to this, an emerging trend is for hotels to form a partnership with a restaurant brand that operates from a designated area within the hotel. This trend is also being seen with bar and coffee **chains** operating outlets within hotel premises.

DEFINITION

Restaurant chains – Businesses that have a similar theme running throughout the operation.

EXAMPLE

A hotel's coffee bar is called 'The Coffee Bean' and is under-performing and losing money. Some of the ongoing costs include staffing, training, equipment maintenance, utilities, space and food and beverage. They identify that many of the customers are actually leaving the hotel and visiting the local Starbucks nearby. The hotel decides to close their coffee bar and outsource this space to another chained coffee chain. Figure 6.5 provides a more in depth example of outsourcing in food and beverage.

(www.litchfieldbeach.com/media/Starbucks2.jpg)

For hotel

Opportunities	▪ Starbucks can provide technical specialisation in coffee service ▪ Less risk of complaints due to a standardised product and quality branded product ▪ Knowledge sharing between partners ▪ Guaranteed monthly rental income from hotel space ▪ Percentage of revenues (depending on agreement) ▪ Attract Starbucks customers to hotel (new income streams) ▪ The hotel can focus on core competences Less capital investment ▪ In design, equipment and facilities ▪ In staffing, training, marketing, advertising and management ▪ Limited costs as these are passed onto operator ▪ Opportunities for cross-marketing
Challenges	▪ 'Change' – new partner ▪ Increased risk due to loss of control ▪ Could potentially lose loyal, existing customers ▪ Negative public relations could impact hotel

BPP LEARNING MEDIA

For partner (Starbucks)

Opportunities	▪ Association with established brand – Brand partnering ▪ New customers ▪ Good location ▪ Cross-marketing
Challenges	▪ Still have costs! ▪ Monthly rental ▪ Acceptance by hotel ▪ Hotel negative PR can affect partner brand

Figure 6.5 Outsourcing food and beverages in hotels

A key element in this type of outsourcing is that both partners must have the same target market.

ACTIVITY 5

Visit some different categories of hotels in your city. Consider different matches of their existing food and beverage outlets with potential chained or branded companies.

7.3 The licensed trade

Public houses (pubs) are establishments licensed for the '*sale of drinks for consumption generally on the premises*' (SIC, 1992), and are a very common and popular part of British culture and tradition. '*There are approximately 61,000 licensed houses in the UK and almost all of them offer food* (*Foskett et al.*, 2008:10). Since the 1990s, food and catering has become a major source of revenue for pubs and '*accounts for approximately 20% of total sales*' (*Foskett et al.*, 2008:13).

Catering in pubs varies greatly from the very simple to the exclusive, and can be divided into four categories:

- **The luxury type restaurant** – where pubs have a separate dining area, offering an extensive menu and wine list.
- **Gastro pubs** – where well-qualified chefs develop menus according to their specialities and using local produce.
- **Speciality restaurants** – where there is a particular theme, such as Mexican, or a certain type of food speciality such as: a carvery, fish or steak.
- **Bar meals** – where food such as sandwiches, burgers and light meals are served from the bar and consumed in the drinking area. Traditional pub dishes may consist of hot pies, fish & chips, gammon & chips and ploughman's.

Trends

Some pubs now rent out their kitchen to a chef who runs the food as a separate business. A pub's core product is beverage so it makes sense to allow another party to operate the food freeing up the landlord to focus on the beverage product and service. The landlord no longer bears the costs associated with running a kitchen and receives a guaranteed rental income irrespective of business levels. The chef is able to be creative and develop menus to suit the clientèle. The pub ultimately benefits as good food will draw customers who will also consume beverages.

Licensing objectives

Throughout the United Kingdom, the sale of alcohol is restricted – pubs, restaurants, shops and other premises must be licensed by the local authority. The individual responsible for the premises must also hold a personal licence. Premises licences, in so far as they concern the sale of alcohol, can be categorised to include on-licences (allowing consumption of alcohol on the premises) and off-licences (alcohol must be removed from the vendor and drunk elsewhere). The age at which people are legally allowed to purchase alcoholic beverages is 18, though children as young as 16 years old can have beer, wine and cider consumed with a table meal in restaurants and pubs under supervision and as long as the drink is purchased by an adult.

Offences under the Licensing Act 2003

There are a number of offences under the Act, some of which are listed below:

- Exposing alcohol for unauthorised sale
- Keeping alcohol on sale for unauthorised sale
- Allowing disorderly conduct on licensed premises
- Sale of alcohol to a person who is drunk
- Obtaining alcohol from a person who is drunk
- Failure to leave licensed premises when asked to do so by an authorised person
- Keeping of smuggled goods

It is a criminal offence for any person to sell alcohol to a person who is under the age of 18 anywhere. There are no exceptions to this.

Source: lgcplus.com

According to the British Beer and Pub Association when the alcohol by volume (abv) is over 0.5% the drink is classed as alcohol for the purpose of licensing law.

Strength of alcoholic drinks

The strength of an alcoholic drink depends on how much alcohol it contains.

The formula for expressing abv on labels is alc. % vol. or % vol. So for a fortified wine, such as sherry or vermouth, labelled as alc. 18% vol. It means that 18% of any given quantity is pure alcohol.

In relation to 'alcohol':

- The alcohol in a drink makes it intoxicating.
- It should be noted, however, that there is no legal definition of the terms 'drunk' or 'drunkenness'.
- Alcohol is classed as a drug because when consumed it alters the physical, mental and emotional state of the drinker.

- Moderate drinking can be part of a healthy lifestyle and often contributes to sociability and relaxation.
- If it is abused, alcohol can have serious negative effects on health and well-being.

Patterns of alcohol abuse

- Binge-drinking is where an individual consumes excessive alcohol in a single session.
- Chronic drinking – is where the individual consumes excessive amounts over an extended period of time on a regular, even a daily basis. Chronic drinking has a negative effect on health (high blood pressure, heart and liver disease and in extreme cases the chronic drinker becomes addicted to the alcohol).

The Weights and Measures Act 1988 requires licensees to dispense beverages according to certain measures.

It is mandatory to display the following notice in ON-Licensed premises.

> The Weights and Measures Act
> (intoxicating Liquor) Order 1988
>
> Unless supplied pre-packed
> WHISKY – GIN – RUM – VODKA
>
> Are offered for sale for
> consumption on these premises
> in quantities of
> TWENTY-FIVE MILLILITRES OR
> MULTIPLES THEREOF

Some countries have restrictions on the sale and consumption of alcohol in relation to religion. Examples include:

- Malaysia
- The Middle East
- Indonesia

CHAPTER SUMMARY

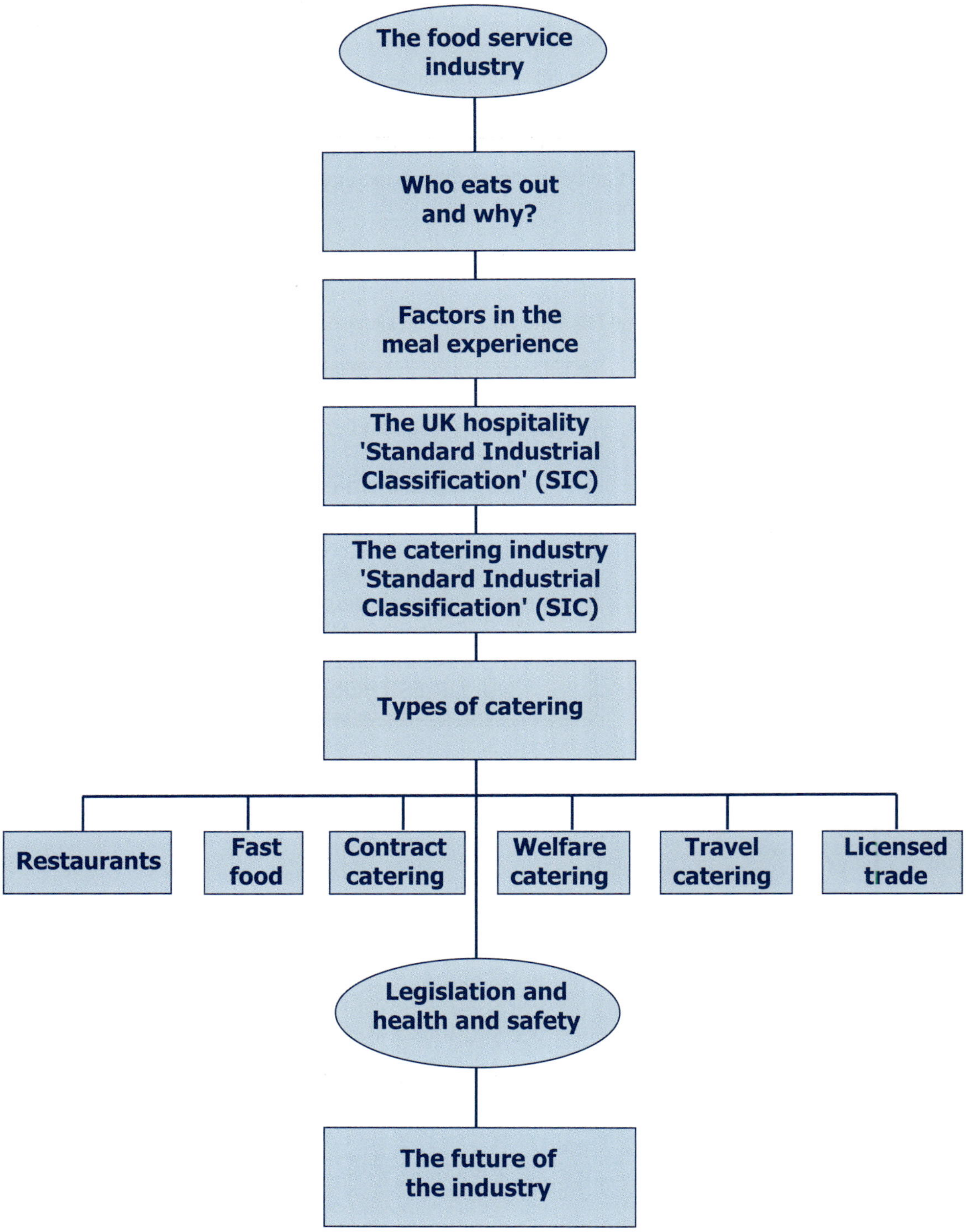

SELF-TEST QUESTIONS

1. *Smith* (1967) states six basic reasons why people eat away from their homes, what are they?
2. List the factors in the meal experience.
3. Identify the different types of catering.
4. Name the three categories of restaurant ownership.
5. *Muller and Woods* (1994) identified five segments of the restaurant market, what are they?
6. What are the four features of fast-food and take-aways?
7. Name the sectors that normally require 'contract catering'.
8. Identify the three employee feeding operations.
9. What sectors does public sector and welfare catering relate to?
10. Identify the areas of travel catering.
11. Catering in pubs can be divided into four categories, what are they?
12. Identify and explain two pieces of legislations relating to catering.

SELF-TEST ANSWERS

1 According to *Smith* (1967), the six reasons why people eat out are: convenience, variety, labour, status, culture/tradition and impulse.

2 The factors in the meal experience are: food, service, cleanliness and hygiene, décor, lighting, air-conditioning, furnishing, acoustics, size and shape of the room, price and clientèle.

3 The different types of catering are: restaurants, fast food outlets, contract catering/employee feeding, welfare catering, travel catering and the licensed trade.

4 The three categories of restaurant ownership are: independent restaurants, chain restaurants and franchises.

5 According to *Muller and Woods* (1994) the five segments of the restaurant market are: quick-service restaurants, mid-scale restaurants, moderate upscale restaurants, upscale restaurants and business dining.

6 The four features of fast-food and take-aways are:

- **Perishability** – the life of the product.
- **Fast product finishing** – from order to the customer consuming the product.
- **Hand/fingers-held product** – can be eaten on the move, ie while walking.
- **Low selling price** – generally fast food is cheap compared with other types of restaurants.

7 The sectors that normally require 'contract catering' include: business and industry, education, healthcare, the military, prisons and transportation.

8 Employee feeding operations include: automatic vending, trolley service and cafeteria operations.

9 Public sector and welfare catering relates to education, healthcare, social care and prisons.

10 The areas of travel catering include: air, rail, road and sea.

11 The four categories of pub catering are:

- The luxury type restaurant
- Gastro pubs
- Speciality restaurants
- Bar meals

12 Two Acts that affect the catering industry are:

- **Health and Safety at Work Act (1974)** This Act has two main aims: to extend the coverage and protection of the law relating to employees and employers and increase awareness of safety among those at work, both employers and employees.

- **Food Labelling Regulations (1984/1999)** The name of the food and list of ingredients, a 'use by' date, storage conditions and conditions of use must be on the label.

ANSWERS TO ACTIVITIES

1 The most popular type of eating outlet in the UK in the year 2000 was the 'Quick Service' restaurant, whereas the least popular was 'Services'.

Between 1996 and 2000: restaurants, quick service, pubs, hotels, staff catering all become more popular; whereas education and services became less popular over the same period.

2 **3** There are no formal answers to these activities as it depends on your own research.

4

	Description	Strengths	Weaknesses
Tray service	Food is prepared in kitchen and placed on either plates or containers and put on trays. All eating utensils and accompaniments are also placed on tray. Food is transported to customers for consumption. Uses: room service or airline catering	Convenient for customer as has complete meal	Food temperature can change during transport
Cafeteria service	Guests move along a counter and make their selection. Some foods are plated, some prepared to order. Collect food on a tray and pay at cashier. Uses: sea catering and work cafeterias	▪ Customers do the work ▪ Promotes other F&B items	Queuing
Drive thru	While in the car customers order through a tannoy system. The food is then prepared and customer collects and pays for food a few minutes later from a window. Customer then drives off with food. Use: Fast food chains such as McDonald's.	Highly convenient for customers as do not have to leave car. Customer occupies no table space leaving more space for other customers.	Food quality can deteriorate
Vending	Customers input money or card to vending machine. Customers make request and collect food from dispatch area. Depending on type of machine the food may be consumed immediately or warmed up in microwave. Uses: Employee cafeteria, budget hotels, non-commercial catering establishments	▪ 24 hours ▪ High control as pre-payment is required before purchase. ▪ Management data available on consumption preferences. ▪ No staff required ▪ Low cost ▪ Less wastage	Machine can malfunction Impersonal Limited choice Electricity Ongoing maintenance Vandalism

	Description	Strengths	Weaknesses
Cocktail	Hot and cold food snacks are placed on large platters in kitchen. Waiters collect platters and walk around offering customers. This method is used mostly where customers are standing and no seating is available. Uses: conference and banquet events, pre-dinner events	Can cater to large numbers	Difficult for employees to move around between customers at times.
Home delivery	Food is ordered through home telephone to food service organisation. Operator takes order and passes to kitchen. On completion, kitchen packs food and food is delivered to customer at required destination or home on transport. Uses: fast food chains and ethnic restaurants	▪ Extends business ▪ Frees up seat capacity	▪ Transport can be unpredictable and delays in delivery due to traffic congestion etc ▪ Food temperature and presentation can deteriorate during transportation ▪ Can deter people from visiting the food and beverage facility directly
Take away	Customer visits or telephones food and beverage operation and places order. Food is prepared and packed. Customer pays for food and takes away food in container or bag. Uses: fast food chains and ethnic restaurants	▪ Extends business ▪ Frees up seat capacity ▪ Brand extension through packaging ▪ Sometimes cheaper for customers	Litter

5 There are no formal answers to this activity as it depends on your own research.

CHAPTER 7

EFFECTIVE QUALITY MANAGEMENT IN THE GLOBAL HOSPITALITY INDUSTRY

Chapter objectives

In this chapter you will:

- Be introduced to the characteristics of service products
- Define service quality
- Investigate technical and functional quality
- Measure and analyse quality standards
- Identify methods of managing quality
- Be introduced to quality standard certifications
- Explain quality consideration in relation to global hospitality
- Be familiar with tools of how to measure quality

Topic list

Definitions of quality
Attributes of service quality
Total Quality Management (TQM)
Quality Standards Certifications
The internationalisation of quality

1 Definitions of quality

Quality is important to all organisations in any sector. Consumers are now more demanding than ever before; organisations must deliver or the savvy customer has plenty of choice to take that business elsewhere. If the consumer is not happy with a product or service they will choose a competing one. Quality gives an organisation a 'competitive advantage' and consequently greater revenue and profit. Bad quality or dangerous goods can lead to legal action, consumers 'suing' companies which inevitably leads to a bad reputation and a loss of business resulting in the organisation's collapse.

DEFINITION

Quality:

'To consistently meet or exceed customer expectations by providing products and services at prices that creates value for customers and profits for the company'. *(Woods & King, 2002)*

'The totality of features and characteristics of a product or service that bear on its ability to satisfy a stated or implied need'. *(British Standards 4778, 1987)*

'Freedom from defects' *(Kotler & Bown, 2003)*

1.1 Characteristics of service products

To be able to understand what quality means in the service sector, first of all we need to understand the characteristics of services. *Evans et al.* (2003) identify four characteristics of service products:

Characteristic	Description
Intangibility	This characteristic refers to service products not being a physical product; you cannot touch these products, as you can a car or a can of soft drink. As you know, services (whether the provision of a holiday or front line customer service), are an experience, and the nature of the experience depends on a number of factors.
Inseparability	**PRODUCTION + CONSUMPTION = INSEPARABILITY** This means that 'production and consumption' occur at the same time, and cannot be separated. Therefore, the person who purchases the 'service product' has direct experience of the production of the service; the product is made at the same time it is being consumed.
Perishability	The service product has a very short life; if it is not consumed then it is lost. (Think about a bottle of milk, if it is not consumed after a few days the milk can no longer be drunk – it is perishable.) Services have a shorter shelf-life even than milk. If the service is not sold at the time of production, the opportunity to sell it is lost. An example would be a hotel room. If the room is not sold for a particular night, then the revenue and usage of that room for that day is lost.
Heterogeneity	Heterogeneity refers to things being 'different'. Services are never identical, despite training by providers which may attempt to standardise levels of service delivery. Individuals with different personalities react in different ways, have alternative up-bringings, diverse cultures, and so it is for service industry staff and customers. For example, a branded hotel in a particular country may not provide the same services or level of service in another country with different cultural perceptions.

Characteristic	Description
Simultaneous production and consumption	The uniqueness of the hospitality product is that, in most cases, it is produced and consumed simultaneously as we saw under 'perishability'. Most manufactured goods are produced in one place, transported and then consumed in another. In outside catering, the product is consumed in another location, but in most circumstances customers must come to the place where it is produced in order to consume it. Mass production is not appropriate as it would require large numbers of customers and producers in one place which would cause environmental, social, cultural and economic problems.
Consistency	Manufactured products are for the most part relatively consistent. Due to the human element of the food and beverage product it is more difficult to achieve **consistency**, which is what some consumers expect and which highly mechanised systems (like fast food chains aim to deliver). Tiredness, emotion, anger can impinge on the delivery of service and in the way the service is received.
No after-sales or guarantees	There is little after-care or service, although usually, feedback is often sought and many hotels now offer loyalty rewards for repeat visits.
No pre trial	With hospitality it is difficult to try the product before consumption: you can't test drive a restaurant or hotel – but recommendations from other good customers and an excellent first impression go a long way!

1.2 Definitions of service quality

Knowles (1994) identifies two approaches to 'service quality':

Approach	Definition
User-based	Under the user-based approach, quality is defined by the user or 'consumer'. It is the difference between what the consumer expects and what the customer experiences. Sometimes a consumer expects 'high-quality' and is disappointed with the actual experience: it is not necessarily a sign of bad quality but may be a sign of mismanaged perceptions (heterogeneity).
Value-based	Quality is related to cost and price. Generally, if something is expensive, we expect 'good quality' and *vice versa*. Price influences to perceptions is important: sometimes very expensive holidays and hotels are expected to live up to the price paid. On the other hand, a more modest hospitality experience can create a pleasant surprise when the quality delivered exceeds the level expected for the price.

FOR DISCUSSION

Have you ever experienced what you thought was 'bad service quality'?

Where was it? Why was it bad quality service in your opinion?

Do you think more expensive 'service products' are better? If so, why?

1.3 Technical and functional quality

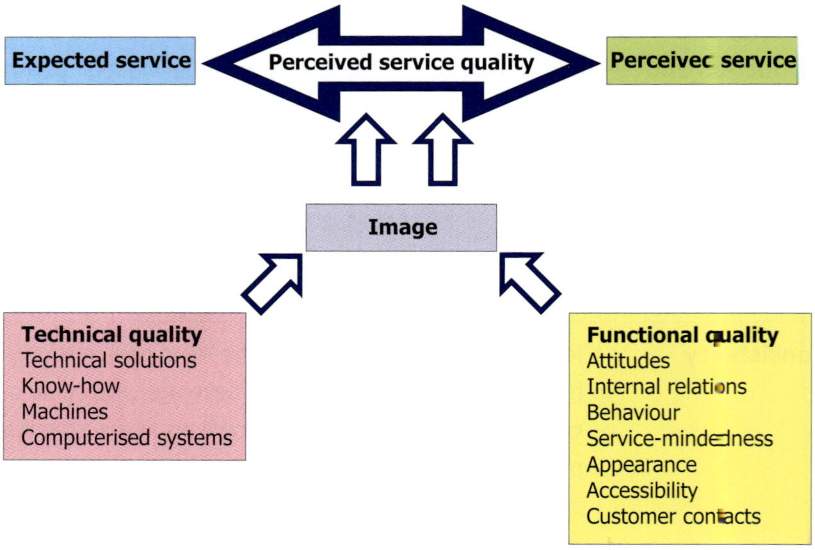

Figure 7.1: Managing the perceived service quality

1.4 Five Gap model

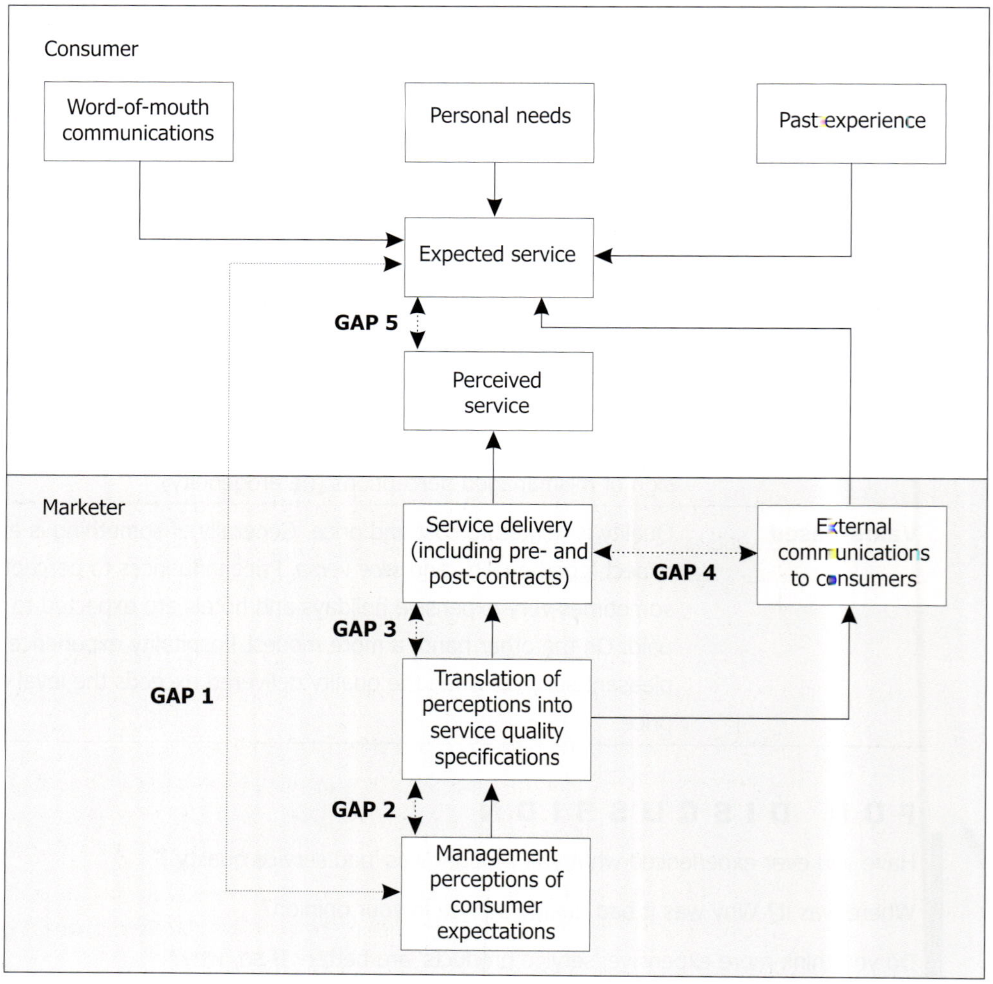

Figure 7.2: Five Gap model

Source: Parasuraman, Zeithaml and Berry

Description of the Five Gap model	
Gap 1	**The gap between management perception and consumer expectation** This relates to the company's service strategy and how it satisfies customer requirements. The company must understand fully its customers' needs and give them what they expect; therefore, a full understanding of the target segment is of great importance. If it is not fully understood – there is a gap. *Example:* Marriott Hotels used to provide bath crystals in its bathrooms, but it was noticed that guests were not using them so they were discontinued. Cable TV increased guest satisfaction – a different and more practical service was appreciated.
Gap 2	**Management perceptions and service specification gap** This occurs when managers know what their customers want, but are unable or unwilling to provide it. There may be numerous reasons: 1. **The company is not committed to service quality** perhaps through cost or a 'product-orientation'. 2. **The company do not see it as 'feasible' to provide this service** – perhaps it is too expensive or it has never been done in the past. 3. **Inadequate task standardisation** – poor co-ordination meaning that the duties are not the same in all hotels may make it difficult to roll out new initiatives. 4. **Absence of goal setting** – organisations may not set goals, or the goals may not be accepted by staff. *Example:* Marriott Hotels developed 'express check-out'. Business guests want to check-out early after breakfast. Traditional check-out took 10–20 minutes often resulting in business guests being late for appointments.
Gap 3	**Service quality specifications and service delivery 'service-performance gap'** This gap occurs when management understand service delivery needs, but employees are unable or unwilling to comply. This can happen in employee-guest interaction, if the employee does not provide a level of service the guest is expecting; such as a warm greeting or a response to a query. This 'gap' may occur due to employees being overworked due to staff shortages, or 'demotivated' staff. To overcome this problem the organisation must first of all find out and then analyse why the guest was dissatisfied. Guests will not always complain so the organisation must seek out ways of encouraging feedback – before the guest takes business elsewhere. It may then be responsibility of the Human Resources (HR) department, to provide more training, hire more appropriate staff, or find ways to motivate employees.
Gap 4	**Service delivery and external communications gap** A gap occurs when an organisation promises more in external communications than it can deliver. This is not only a problem in terms of the organisation's service delivery, but has legal implications. In the UK organisations must adhere to **The Trade Descriptions Act** (1968) which states that descriptions must be 'truthful and accurate', and **The Supply of Goods & Services Act** (1982: amended 1994) which states that whatever service is provided it must be done with 'reasonable skill and care'. For example, if literature provided to guests states that an on-site restaurant is available, such as an 'on-site' restaurant, the restaurant must be open when guests visit even if it is low season. If it isn't, this could lead to guest dissatisfaction and potentially legal action.

Description of the Five Gap model	
Gap 5	**The gap between expected service and perceived service** This gap relates to the difference between what was expected and what was perceived in the guest's mind; the technical and functional qualities of the delivery. If the guest receives a worse service than they were expecting, then they are dissatisfied, on the other hand, a good quality service may match or ideally exceed customer expectations.

FOR DISCUSSION

Have you ever been 'dissatisfied' by the delivery of a service?

Why were you dissatisfied?

Have you ever been surprised by the delivery of customer service?

Why were you surprised?

2 Attributes of service quality

Attributes of service quality are very important to any service provider, but most particularly to the very competitive hospitality sector. If companies concern themselves with the attributes of service quality, this can lead to a competitive advantage over others. By exceeding customer expectations, customers return and increase profits for the company.

Attributes	Description
Tangibles	'**The physical evidence of the service**' This includes: ▪ **Physical facilities**: such as the building, is it clean, attractive, well laid out and safe? ▪ **Appearance of personnel**: are the staff well-groomed? ▪ **Equipment** to provide the service: is it safe, well maintained and adequate for the task?
Reliability	'**Consistency of performance and dependability**' ▪ **The company performs the service right the first time** ▪ **The firm delivers what is promised** ▪ **Accuracy** – billing, record keeping, given service at the designated time, eg wake up call
Responsiveness	'**The willingness or readiness of employees to provide the service**' ▪ **Prompt willing service** ▪ **Dealing with a query** ▪ **Appear available to help**
Assurance	'**The knowledge and courtesy of employees and their ability to convey trust and confidence**' ▪ **Company reputation** ▪ **Confidentiality** ▪ **Knowledge of staff** ▪ **Financial and personal security**
Empathy	'**The provision of caring individualised attention to customers**' ▪ Recognising regular customers ▪ Learning individual needs and requirements ▪ Customised service

FOR DISCUSSION

Using the attributes of service quality, have you ever experienced an occasion when one or more of the service quality attributes was not achieved? For example, a hotel was dirty, or a bill was incorrect.

What happened in this situation? Did you complain? How did the hotel or service provider respond?

3 Total Quality Management (TQM)

DEFINITION

'The participation of all members of an organisation in improving processes, products, services, and the culture in which they work.' (www.mariosalexandrou.com)

As we can determine from the definition, TQM must involve everyone in the workplace and every aspect of the organisation.

3.1 Elements of TQM

There are six elements of TQM and all of these elements are interrelated and integral within the whole organisation, as illustrated below.

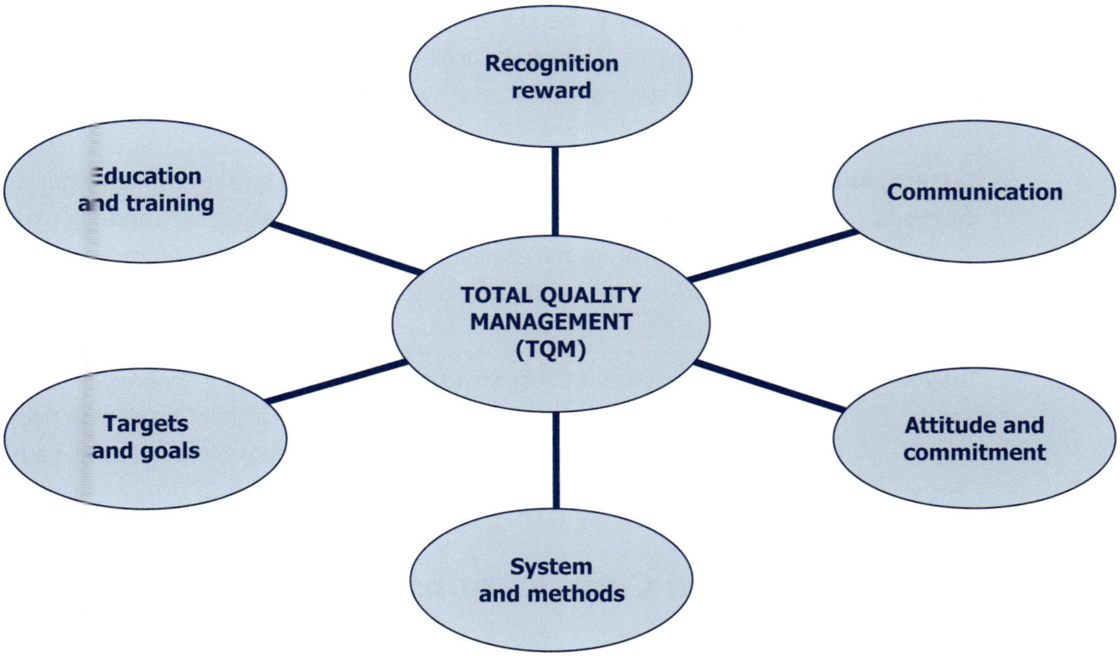

Figure 7.3: The six elements of TQM

Total Quality Management	
Recognition reward	This relates to recognising staff for achievements, and acknowledging that their hard work and commitment has been noticed. It must apply to all staff and must not be 'discriminatory'. Any member of staff from directors of the board to the cleaners, can be acknowledged for their effort and achievements. This can prove very motivating for staff, and may involve financial rewards in the form of a bonus, acknowledgement from 'a pat on the back' or an 'employee of the month award' or a gift of some kind, such as a free holiday, or in the case of a hotel company free room nights.

Total Quality Management	
Education and training	In TQM education and training allows all employees the opportunity to gain skills and knowledge in relation to their job and their career within the organisation. Generally, organisations provide 'in-house' training for staff members, allowing employees the opportunity to improve performance, knowledge and techniques within their work environment. Some organisations may help staff obtain external qualifications, relevant to their job or career ladder. Education and training not only helps in improving performance due to skills and knowledge gained, it can also prove very motivating for staff, which in turn can improve the quality of their work.
Communication	TQM allows for vertical and horizontal communication, ie communication is not only from the top-down, but also across departments and from the bottom-up. Staff who are encouraged to input their ideas and views may have greater insights because of their direct contact with customers. Open-door policies, which allow employees to directly communicate with their bosses, are helpful as barriers to communication are eliminated.
Attitude and commitment	Everyone in the organisation has to work towards the same goals and objectives – therefore, everyone in the organisation should have a culture of trying to improve performance. This can be achieved by on-going education, staff training and internal communication, and by allowing all members of staff a 'voice' if they so desire.
Systems and methods	Consistent and recognised processes have to be implemented if quality standards are to be improved throughout the whole organisation. These processes must identify, analyse and eliminate what is causing poor performance – 'the quality system' – and a certification of standards can be a way of achieving TQM standards.
Targets and goals	Strategic goals and objectives need to be constantly reviewed and monitored so standards are maintained. If there is a loss of sight of these objectives and goals, then there is no synergy and cohesion in the organisation and all parts of the organisation will lose their direction and scope.

4 Quality Standard Certifications

British Standard 5750

Established in 1979, initially for manufacturing industries, BS 5750 was applied to many organisations in varying sectors to '*assess the suitability of their supplier's products*', and to establish the provision of a certain quality of goods and services.

Part 2 of the Standard relates to the provision of services, therefore the hotel and catering industry is included in this part, and it sets out that services must be provided to a certain specification or standard.

ISO 9000 Series

In 1994 BS EN ISO 9002 was introduced '*to identify the systems, procedures, and criteria that ensure that a product or service meets customer requirements*', (*Foskett et al.*, 2008) to establish parity of British standards with international standards.

Visit the following websites to find out more about quality.

Investors in People

http://www.investorsinpeople.co.uk
Information about the Investors in People scheme

Hospitality Assured

www.hospitalityassured.com
Information about the Hospitality Assured quality scheme

British Standards Institute

http://www.bsi-global.com/
Information about ISO 9001 –put ISO 9001 in the search function on this page to go to the relevant information.

4.1 Key elements in quality management

Management responsibility	Policy, objectives, identification of key personnel
Quality system procedures	All functions must be covered
Auditing the system	Must be audited internally
Quality in marketing	Honest promotional activities
Material control and supply chains	Supplies must be traceable
Non-conformity	Ensuring that faulty products/services do not reach the customer
Corrective action	Identify reasons for faults and implement measures to correct them
After-sales service	Procedures for monitoring quality of after-sales service
Documentation and records	Records of inspections, actions and audit reports
Personnel and training	Identifying needs, provision and verification of training
Product safety and liability	Procedures for handling, storing and processing materials, eg foods

4.2 Quality management excellence model

The following figure shows the enablers, that is, the leadership, people, policies and partnerships which achieve results. The organisation must evaluate these results and learn from them, and where they fail to meet expectation, develop new processes and systems to address the flaws.

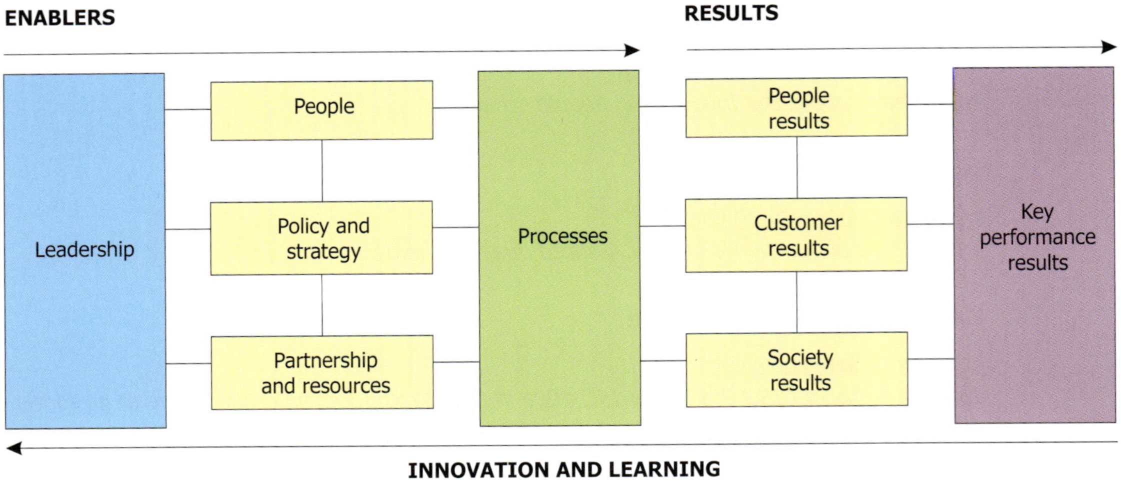

Figure 7.4: European Foundation for quality management excellence model (1999)

5 The internationalisation of quality

The internationalisation of the hotel industry has presented new challenges and opportunities with regard to quality.

Culture

Source: leaningtowardsjustice

Gee (1994) explains 'culture is important within the hotel environment for the following five reasons

- In communicating, transacting business, and negotiating with colleagues from other countries.
- In working for a foreign-based hotel company.
- In managing human resources in another country, whether the employees are indigenous to that country or hired from yet another country.
- In managing foreign born or culturally diverse workers in the domestic hospitality industry.
- In accommodating international guests.'

The international hotel guest

With the increase in travel, destinations are now required to prepare for guests from all over the world who have specific cultural needs.

'International hospitality organisations will have to engage in greater degrees of customisation. Product/services will have to be tailored to meet individual needs and tastes' (Welch, 1994)

EXAMPLE

A guest from Saudi Arabia is travelling to London and staying three nights in a hotel. In this situation the hotel should consider the following:

- As a Muslim, alcohol should be removed from the mini bar.
- Room employees should be aware of the direction of Mecca to advise the customer for when praying.
- The Bible (if the standard) should be removed from the bedroom.
- Information on local Mosques should be available.

Gee (1994) says international travellers travel with their own cultural baggage full of expectations, values, preferences, and habits. In receiving foreign guests, hotels are often faced with the challenge of reconciling local hospitality traditions with the home traditions of their guests.

FOR DISCUSSION

Consider you are a member of the management team in a hotel hosting a conference that is attracting international guests staying within the hotel. Consider some of the needs of the following nationalities, as listed below and what the hotel can do to accommodate those needs.

Guest	Nationality
Mr Schneider	North America
Mr Tanaka	Japan
Mrs Elan	Israel
Mr Meyer	Germany

(Feedback for this discussion activity is provided at the end of the Chapter)

Gee (1994) highlights some of the services that hotels can provide to accommodate international hotel guests as illustrated in the following figure.

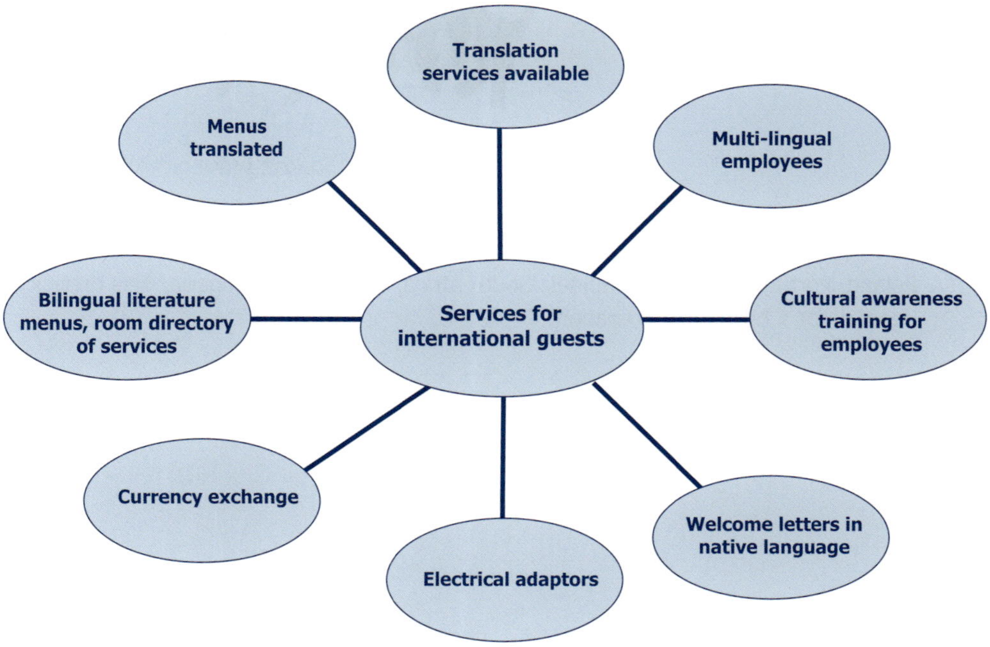

Figure 7.5: Services for international guests

ACTIVITY 1 — 10 minutes

Identify some of the following international signs used within the hospitality industry

International hotel employees

Source: www.nithikorn.com/images/expatriate.png

Hotel workforces now tend to be much more homogenous due to individuals migrating and travelling to new countries. In London hotels it is likely that you will find employees from countries such as Germany, Poland, Portugal, Brazil, Philippines, South Africa, Australia and Nigeria. This diversity provides many benefits for a hospitality operation.

The advantages of international employees for an organisation

Figure 7.6: Advantages of international employees for an organisation

Hotels can accommodate international employees and achieve a higher standard of employee by:

- Taking time to learn about their cultures and backgrounds
- Taking note of dates of cultural or religious importance
- Providing meals that are more familiar to them whenever possible
- Providing language lessons to assist with development and to improve internal communication
- Provide facilities for them to communicate with home

'Marriott's commitment to global diversity is absolute. Our determination to provide opportunities for our associates and clientele is one of the main reasons people want to work and do business with us.'

J.W. Marriott, Jr., Chairman and CEO

Expatriate employment

The hotel industry provides many opportunities for individuals to travel and work. Many international hotel companies will employ managers from outside their countries. For example, many hotels in the Middle East and Far East will have European and North American Executive Chefs, Food & Beverage Directors and General Managers. A common expatriate package for such positions may include:

- Tax-free salary
- Salary in currency of individual's home country
- Furnished accommodation
- Flights

Advantages for hotel	Challenges for hotel
Fresh ideas and approaches	Expensive contract
Internationalises the team	Requires more assistance due to unfamiliarity
Knowledge transfer	High risk due to new environment
	Cultural mistakes

Advantages for expatriate	Challenges for expatriate
Opportunities to travel	Adaptation to new environment
Opportunities to meet new people	Adaptation to new culture
Gaining an insight into a new environment and culture	Missing family and friends
Demonstrates flexibility and adaptability enhances job prospects	Language challenges
New knowledge	Gaining acceptance
More culturally aware	

Figure 7.7: Expatriate employment: opportunities and challenges

blog.moveone.info

Torrington and Hall (1991) cited in *Jones & Pizam* (1994) describe management development as concerned with developing the whole person in order to enhance their performance work. This is particularly relevant for the international manager, where business education and cultural awareness are as significant as technical job skills.

To reduce the possibility of failure companies put employees on a pre-acculturation course before their departure. This includes (as detailed by *Gee* (1994)):

- Social and business etiquette (and protocol)
- History and folklore
- Current affairs
- Values of the host culture
- Geography, climate, and the physical environment
- Sources of pride: artists, musicians, things to see and do
- Religion (extremely important in Islamic countries)
- Political structure
- Legal structure
- Economic structure
- General business conditions
- Prevailing business practices
- Practical matters – currency, transportation, time zones, hours of business
- Religious facts/Key holidays
- Cultural norms
- Some key words in language

According to *Gee* (1994): protocol – that is sets of unwritten guidelines or rules for the conduct of business and business dining and entertaining – is present in every culture. It is important that hoteliers know and practise the protocol for several reasons.

- To show respect
- To avoid embarrassment
- To enhance understanding, and
- To avoid dealing from a weakened position in negotiating.

EXAMPLE

In China when giving and receiving business cards you use both hands.

ACTIVITY 2 **Homework**

List down any types of business protocol for your country that would be useful for an expatriate to know before commencing employment.

FOR DISCUSSION

Consider which countries (if any) you would like to work in. Discuss why and the specific challenges and benefits that may be encountered specific to those countries.

Expatriate assignment cycle

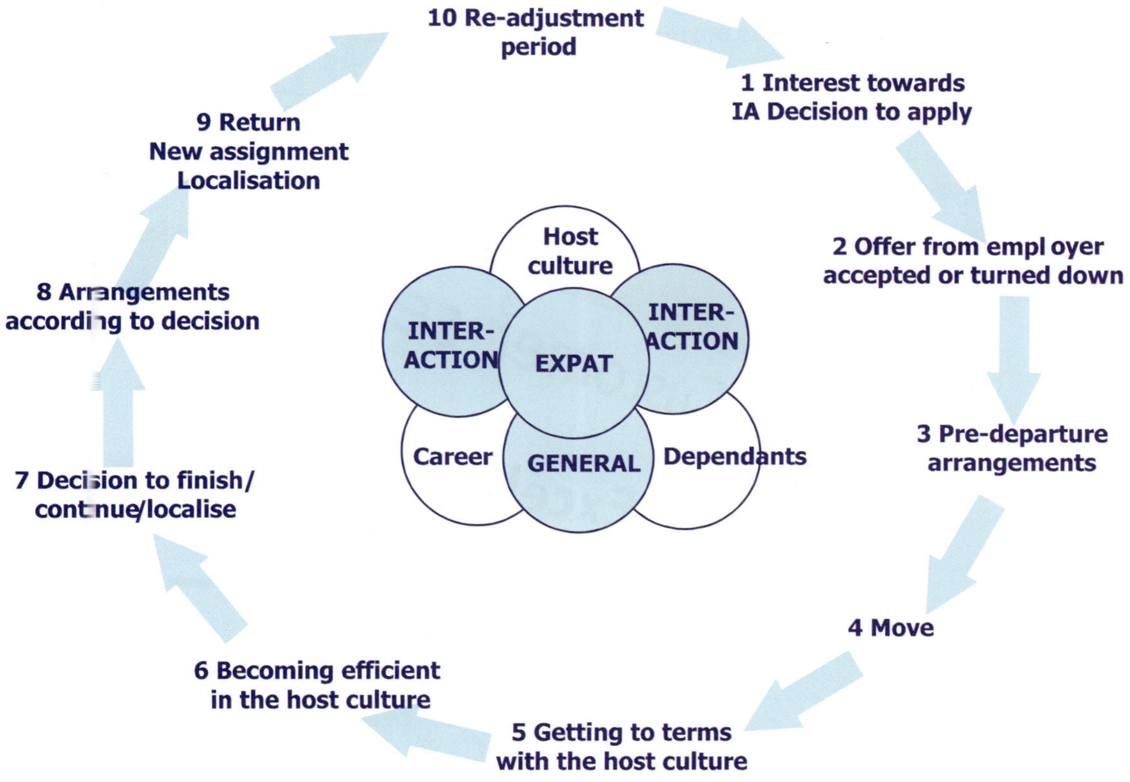

Figure 7.8: Expatriate assignment cycle

Quality standards

Standards of Performance or 'Standard Operating Procedures' (SOPs)

To assist with meeting customers' needs and wants, standards of performance have to be created and implemented.

'Standards of Performance help with consistency because they detail exactly what must be done and how it should be done'. *Ninemeir* (2000)

Advantages of performance standards for an operation

- Consistency of service
- Guides the employees in their work
- Supervisory tool for training employees
- Supervisory tool for evaluating employee performance
- Management tool for measuring performance against competitors
- Assists in allocating costs per task accurately

Examples of standards in a food and beverage operation may include:

- How to clean cutlery
- How to taking a pre-dinner reservation
- How to take a table booking over the telephone
- How to complete a charge using a 'Point of Sale' machine
- How to open wine
- How to welcome a customer
- How to carry plates
- How to deal with complaints

Major hotel chains such as Hilton and Holiday Inn have large directories of standards that are created to be implemented their hotels worldwide, be it in Mumbai, Sydney or London. These standards ensure that international customers can expect the same level of service in each hotel.

Quality monitoring and measurement

When an organisation has implemented quality tools to achieve quality products and service it is vital to measure the success of the organisation in achieving quality (or not).

Source: www.getentrepreneurial.com/images/customer%20service.jpg

Leaders committed to quality must ensure that there are tools in place to measure their staff member's efforts at providing great service to guests. *Woods & King* (2002)

Monitoring and measuring quality can be carried out in different ways. One way an organisation can approach this is by conducting research internally and externally.

Wuest cited in *Kandampully et al.* (2001) *'The service encounter and the customer's evaluation of the quality of this service encounter are critical to service business success'.*

Second data (industry magazines or reports)	**Mystery guests**	**Observation (management by walking around)**
External surveys (e-mail, mail or telephone surveys)	**Management information (popular/unpopular items)**	**Critical log books (comments by departmental supervisors and staff relating to the operation)**
Focus groups (inviting a group of customers or members of the public to gather information on needs and wants)	**Face-to-face feedback (speaking to customers to establish satisfaction)**	**Customer questionnaires**

CHAPTER SUMMARY

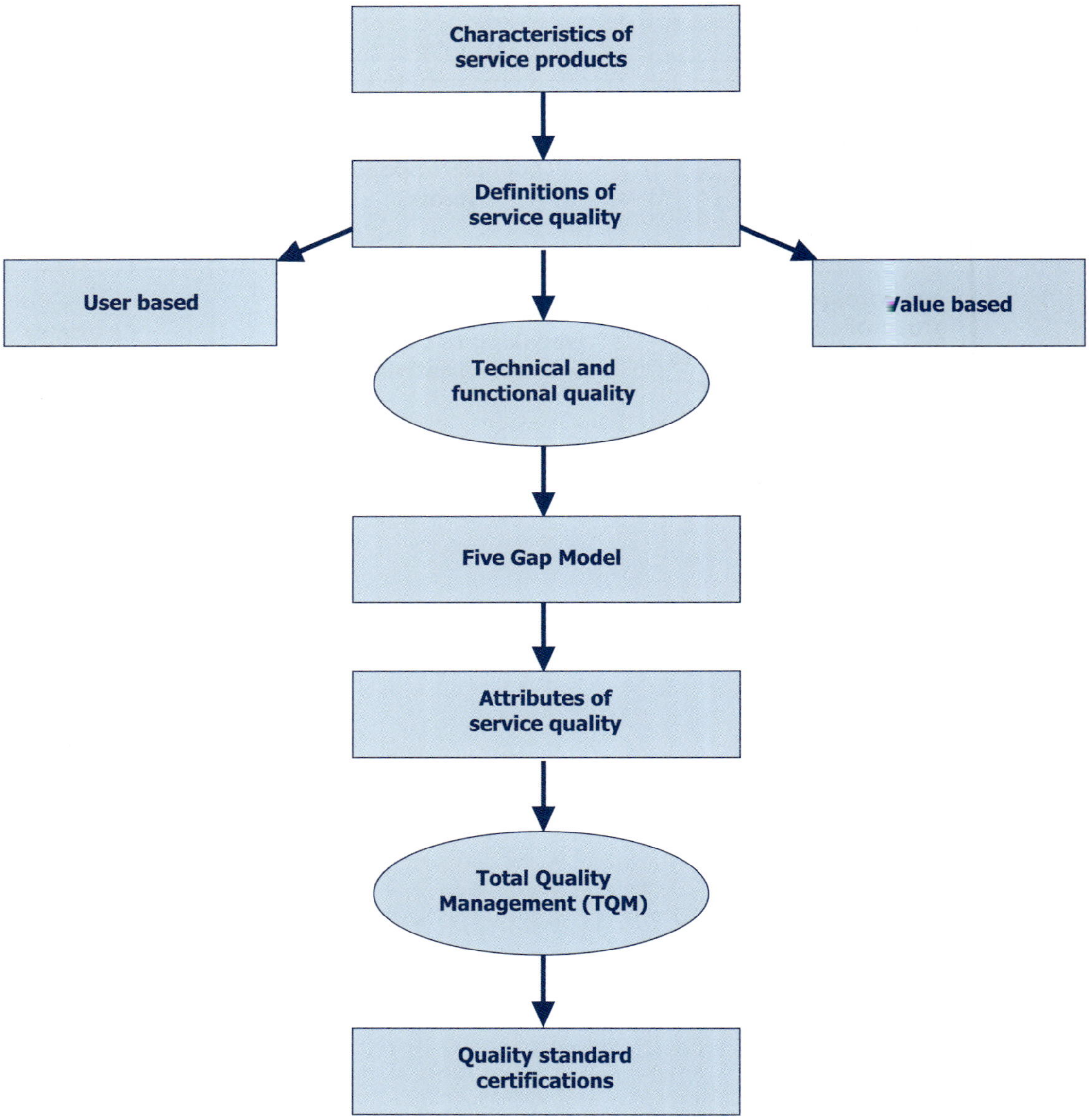

SELF-TEST QUESTIONS

1. Identify the four characteristics of service products (*Evans et al.*, 2003).
2. What are the two definitions of service quality according to *Knowles* (1994)?
3. List the five gaps in the '5 Gap Model'.
4. Identify the attributes of service quality.
5. What does TQM mean?
6. List the six elements of TQM.
7. List the key elements in quality management in the hotel and catering industry of the ISO 9000 series.
8. What are the enablers of the European Foundation for quality management excellence model (1999)?
9. What are the results of the European Foundation for quality management excellence model (1999)?

SELF-TEST ANSWERS

1 The four characteristics of service products are:

- **Intangibility**: the experience is something we cannot touch.
- **Inseparability**: production and consumption happen at the same time, 'the service factory'.
- **Perishability**: if the product is not sold, the sale is lost.
- **Heterogeneity**: no experience is the same, due to different personalities etc.

2 According to *Knowles* (1994) the two definitions of service quality are: user-based and value-based.

3 The five Gaps in the '5 Gap model' are:

Gap 1 The gap between the management perception and the consumer expectation.

Gap 2 Management perceptions and service specification gap.

Gap 3 Service quality specifications and service delivery 'service-performance gap'.

Gap 4 Service delivery and external communications gap.

Gap 5 The gap between expected service and perceived service.

4 The attributes of service quality are: tangibles, reliability, responsiveness, assurance and empathy.

5 TQM stands for total quality management.

6 The six elements of TQM are: recognition reward, education and training, communication, attitude and commitment, systems and methods, targets and goals.

7 The key elements in quality management in the hotel and catering industry of the ISO 9000 series are:

- Management responsibility
- Quality system procedures
- Auditing the system
- Quality in marketing
- Material control and traceability
- Non-conformity
- Corrective action
- After-sales service
- Documentation and records
- Personnel and training
- Product safety and liability

8 The enablers are: leadership, people, policy and strategy, partnership and resources and processes.

9 The results are: people results, customer results, society results and key performance results.

Feedback to discussion

Guest	Cultural needs
Mr Schneider – American	Larger bedrooms Friendly, personalised service Iced tap water in room Sightseeing information
Mr Tanaka – Japanese	Translator (available if required) Green tea in room Japanese food available or information on local Japanese dining Shopping information
Mrs Elan – Israel	A customer from Israel may require kosher food. Therefore, the hotel should have contacts for local Kosher restaurants or supermarkets. Orthodox customers may create further challenges during Shabbat where they may have specific requests.
Mr Meyer – Germany	Customers tend to require fast, efficient service

ANSWERS TO ACTIVITIES

1 International signage answers

Telephone	Mail	Currency exchange	First aid	Lost and found
Baggage lockers	Elevator	Toilets, Men	Toilets, Women	Toilets
Information	Hotel information	Taxi	Bus	Ground transportation
Rail transportation	Air transportation	Heliport	Water transportation	
Car rental	Restaurant	Coffee shop	Bar	Shops
Ticket purchase	Baggage check-in	Baggage claim	Customs	Immigration
No smoking	Smoking	No parking	Parking	No entry

2 There are no formal answers to this activity as it depends on your own research.

PRACTICE EXAMINATION

This is a real past CTH examination. Once you have completed your studies, you should attempt this under exam conditions. That means allowing yourself the full time available of 2½ hours. Do not look at the suggested answers until you have finished.

QUESTION PRACTICE

CTH diploma courses are all assessed by examination. This method of assessment is used as it is considered to be the fairest method to ensure that students have learnt the things they have been taught.

On the following pages you will find a practice exam for this subject. When you have worked through this Study Guide and answered the self-test questions you should make a full attempt at the practice exam, preferably in exam conditions. This will give you the opportunity to practise questions in the CTH exam format.

The exam questions in this paper are examples of this subject's questions. The answers provided are notes used by the examiners when marking the exam papers. They are not complete specimen answers but are of the type and style expected. In some cases there is a list of bullet points and in others more text or essay-style, however they are representative of the content expected in your responses. Information given contains the main points required by the Chief Examiner.

SECTION 1 – A1-A10 (2 mark questions)

These questions are looking for factual information and test concise and logical thinking. As a general rule for a two mark question CTH is looking for one or two word answers or maybe a short sentence. Therefore either text or bullet points will be accepted. If two points are asked for marks will be allocated for each point. If only one answer is asked for we would expect a short sentence.

Here we are trying to assess your knowledge of the subject and to identify if you can recall the basic principles, methods, techniques and terminology linked to the subject.

SECTION 2 – A11-A15 (4 mark questions)

These questions are looking for factual information and test concise and logical thinking. As a general rule CTH is looking for bullet points or a short paragraph for the answer to a four mark question. If two or four points are asked for marks will be allocated for each point. If only one answer is asked for we would expect a few sentences or a short paragraph.

Here we are trying to assess your knowledge of the subject and to identify if you understand and can demonstrate how principles, methods and techniques can be used.

SECTION 3 – B1 (20 mark questions)

These 20 mark questions are looking for factual information and how those facts can be applied to both the subject and the hospitality industry. We expect to see essay-style answers to show your knowledge of the subject and its application.

From this section you need to select three questions from a choice of five. **Do not answer more than three as only the first three answers will be marked.** These are essay-style questions so you should select the three that you feel you are the most prepared for. No matter how good the answer is if it does not answer the question you will not be given any marks – marks are only allocated when the answer matches the question.

If you run out of time in the exam jot down the essential points that you intended to include, the examiner will allocate marks for any correct information given.

It is difficult to assess how much you are required to write for a 20 mark question – some people can answer in a page, other people need several pages. What is important is that you answer the question asked – it is about the quality of the answer not the quantity written.

20 mark questions

The following descriptors give you information on the CTH marking scheme and what you need to aim for at each level.

Grade	Explanation
Level 4 (15-20)	Demonstrates knowledge of analysis and evaluation of the subject
Level 3 (11-15)	Demonstrates knowledge of application of the subject
Level 2 (6-10)	Demonstrates knowledge and comprehension of the subject
Level 1 (1-5)	Does not demonstrate knowledge and understanding of the subject

Hospitality finance

It is important to show all your working out in questions involving calculations. Marks will be awarded for correct workings even if the final answer is incorrect.

Level descriptors

The following level descriptors give you information on what you need to aim for at each grade.

Grade	Explanation
Distinction	Demonstrates knowledge of analysis and evaluation of the subject
Merit	Demonstrates knowledge of application of the subject
Pass	Demonstrates knowledge and comprehension of the subject
Fail	Does not demonstrate knowledge and understanding of the subject

EXAMINATION

CTHCM Diploma in Hotel Management

Subject: **The Global Hospitality Industry (DHM 192)**

Series: **January 2008**

Time Allowed: **2.5 hours**

Instructions:

You are allowed **TEN MINUTES** to read through this examination paper before the commencement of the examination. Please read the questions carefully, paying particular attention to the marks allocated to each question or part of a question, and taking account of any special instructions or requirements laid down in any of the questions.

This Examination Paper contains **TWO SECTIONS.**
Answer **ALL** questions in **Section A**
Answer any **THREE** questions in **Section B**

On completion of your examination:

Make sure that your name, CTHCM membership number, and centre number are clearly marked at the top of each answer sheet and on any other material you hand in.

Marks Allocation

Section A = 40% of the module grade
Section B = 60% of the module grade

SECTION A

*Answer **all** questions in this section. This section carries a total of **40** marks.*

A1. Describe two positive effects of the increased use of technology on a hotel. *(2 marks)*

A2. What is the main function of the hospitality and catering industry? *(2 marks)*

A3. Discuss four influences that contribute to deciding on the location of a hotel. *(2 marks)*

A4. What is the difference between a boutique hotel and a chain hotel? *(2 marks)*

A5. Name two external economic influences that can have an effect on the hospitality and catering industry. *(2 marks)*

A6. Apart from providing meals at work, give four other places where contract caterers operate. *(2 marks)*

A7. Give two situations where food production and food service are separated. *(2 marks)*

A8. What is meant by the term welfare catering? *(2 marks)*

A9. Give two reasons why most countries have government restrictions on the sale of alcohol. *(2 marks)*

A10. What is a food court? *(2 marks)*

A11. Name four main differences between a city centre hotel and a resort hotel. *(4 marks)*

A12. Explain how airport hotels cater for a number of different sections of the airport and airline passenger market. *(4 marks)*

A13. What is Yield Management? *(4 marks)*

A14. Give four features of fast food outlets that make them different to other catering outlets. *(4 marks)*

A15. As society changes so the hospitality industry has to change. Give an example of this that relates to eating and drinking habits in a destination you know. *(4 marks)*

SECTION B

*Answer any __**3**__ questions in this section. Each question carries a total of __**20**__ marks.*

B1.

a) Branded hotels are increasingly dominating the hotel industry. Using your own examples, clearly explain how this benefits both the customer and the owner. *(14 marks)*

b) What are the advantages to hotels in joining consortia? *(6 marks)*

B2.

Transport catering (road, rail, air and sea) is distinguished from other food and beverage catering by a number of characteristics. Discuss these characteristics and give examples from your own experience to illustrate your answer. *(20 marks)*

B3.

Describe the positive and negative contributions to the international hospitality industry made by the emergence of multinational hotel groups. *(20 marks)*

B4.

a) What is contract catering? *(2 marks)*

b) List four ways that a client of a catering contractor can measure performance. *(8 marks)*

c) There are various types of contracts that can be used in contract catering. Provide an explanation of two of these. *(10 marks)*

B5.

Budget Hotels have seen major growth over recent years.

a) Give a definition of a Budget Hotel. *(2 marks)*

b) Discuss the factors which have led to the development of Budget Hotels. *(10 marks)*

c) Budget Hotels are generally in prime locations. Discuss the reasons for this. *(8 marks)*

PRACTICE EXAMINATION ANSWERS

SECTION A

A1 Computer reservation systems, corporate guest history, faster check-in, check-out, electronic security system, voicemail handling service, purchasing system, wake-up systems, remote sales and marketing system, web distribution.

A2 To sell the use of accommodation in the form of rooms for sleeping or other purposes such as conferences and business meetings. To sell meals usually for consumption on the premises.

or

To provide overnight accommodation for people staying away from home, and sustenance for people eating away from home or not preparing their own meals.

A3 Location of access roads, availability of supplies, staff, surrounding area (outstanding natural beauty, airports etc).

A4 A boutique hotel is totally individual. Everything within the hotel will not be seen in another hotel including décor, room style etc.

A chain hotel will often have a similar layout, décor, room style etc are standardised. Toiletries, matches, signage, key cards etc are the same in all hotels and will have the same logo. Service is also standardised.

A5 The state of the world economy
Exchange rates
Interest rates

A6 Schools, hospitals, prisons, army, healthcare, business and industry, education, military, and transportation.

A7 Sous-vide, cook-chill, cook-freeze, airline catering, railway catering, any other example.

A8 The provision of meals for those who are unable to provide for themselves, inability resulting from age, both the very young and the elderly, illness and other type of infirmity. Includes food service in education (schools, colleges, universities); healthcare (public and private hospitals) and social care (prisons, care homes, day centres, meals on wheels).

In welfare catering the costs are kept to a tight budget, nutrition and a balanced diet are of major importance, it is not for profit, it keeps production and service costs to a minimum. Most welfare catering does not involve an exchange of money and can be done in a centralised kitchen and meals distributed to different locations such as schools.

A9 Revenue protection, protection of minors/children, prevent criminals being involved, to protect the public from being cheated by unscrupulous vendors.

A10 A food court is a type of plaza (indoor or outdoor) with adjoining counters of multiple food vendors and providing a common area for self-serve dining. Food courts may be found in shopping malls and airports, and in various regions, such as Asia and Africa, may be a stand alone development.

A11 The answer needs to show how a city centre hotel is mainly for business users, especially from Monday to Friday, whereas a resort hotel is for leisure.

Resort hotel has more leisure facilities such as golf, horse riding, tennis courts perhaps in the countryside or by the sea, dining is more relaxed, possibly more informal atmosphere, guests stay for more than one night possibly a week or more, it may be seasonal, may be bargain breaks out of season, inclusive package deals, no shows and walk-ins rarely happen. People book well in advance.

City centre hotels tend to be used by business people, may be just one night stay, high room rate Monday to Thursday, business centre, express check-in/check-out, self check-in/check-out, chauffer service, airport service, more formal atmosphere, internet and fax access in rooms, business/meeting rooms available, conference facilities, quick and speedy service, voice mail.

A12 Shops, coffee shops, bars, restaurants, airline catering, provision for delays, accommodation, day lets and short-term lets.

A13 Yield management, also known as revenue management, is the process of understanding, anticipating and reacting to consumer behaviour in order to maximise revenue or profits. Firms that engage in yield management usually use computer yield management systems to do so. The internet has greatly facilitated this process. Yield management can result in price discrimination, where a firm charges customers consuming otherwise identical goods or services a different price for doing so.

Yield management is particularly suitable when selling perishable products, ie goods that become unsellable at a point in time (for example bedrooms or air tickets just after a flight takes off). Industries that use yield management include airlines, hotels, stadiums and other venues with a fixed number of seats, and advertising.

A14

- A finished product shelf life of usually minutes and on occasions, hours. Rapid deterioration occurs beyond these times particularly without holding equipment. This perishability factor is consistent with that of service products generally.
- Fast product finishing (and in some cases total production) and service times. The range of fast foods, demand levels, production methods and system efficiencies mean that actual times will differ from between 2 to about 15 minutes for products provided to consumers on-site to about 30 minutes for those delivered to consumers off-site.
- A hand- or finger-held product often accompanied with disposable packaging and sometimes disposable cutlery.
- A low selling price relative to other restaurant products.
- Because of its nature fast food can be consumed on or off the premises as a take-away or a delivered product.

A15 Changes in licensing law, healthy eating, technological advances, fast food and home delivery, increased leisure time, people living longer or any other example. Students need to identify a cause and explain how this affects customer habits.

SECTION B

B1 (a) To the customer, the best brands convey a warrant of quality. Strong brands offer consistency of product from one property to another. A brand name may offer the advantage of charging a premium price over equivalent offers from rival companies, gaining market share against these rivals, keeping customers loyal to the brand. In many cases the popularity of branded operations has pushed established operators to develop and internationalise their chains further. Economies of scale is a clear advantage of large chains.

- The brand gives an image of the hotel and this provides customers with assurance that the hotel is good.
- It encourages customer loyalty as the customer knows that the brand is good. This gives the hotel repeat business.
- The hotel need not undertake as much marketing as the brand is recognised by the customers. This cuts operating costs for the hotel.
- Loyal customers get special discounts and promotions and if they are satisfied they bring more loyal customers to the hotel and this means more business for the hotel.
- Through brands customers can recognise the hotel easily even in other countries. This will give guests familiarity with the brand and bring business back to the establishment.
- More branded hotels give consumers more choices and variety. This will turn create competition for one another resulting in hotel being better managed and provide a better service. It benefits the hotel as the hotel is striving for the best.

(b) For smaller and/or individual hotel properties which cannot compete against the far greater budgets and reach of the major brands and lack a global reservation system, the solution of joining a consortium is advisable. The advantages of joint purchasing and marketing activities can be greater than the 'cost' of giving up an element of independence.

There are several advantages to hotels joining consortia, especially small hotels.

- Through bulk purchasing by the consortia, the hotel saves cost of materials.
- By undertaking marketing activities together, the hotel cuts marketing costs and also reaches out to more customers.
- The hotel will have a support in times of difficulty through the consortia.
- The hotel will be informed of events happening in the industry through the consortia. Update on certain trends in the industry.
- The hotel can get professional advice on operating the hotel through the consortia.
- Able to reach out to more guests as, if one hotel in the consortia is fully booked, they will send guests to another hotel nearby which is in the consortia.

B2 Rail, airline, road and ship catering differ in terms of the types of food they offer and the systems they use to provide the service but they have many factors in common. In particular, passengers who are travelling long distances cannot make the same choices about where to eat or drink that are open to people travelling by private car. Organisations also have the operational constraints of providing staff and raw materials to a unit which moves from one location to another. This requires a sophisticated logistic planning system for the allocation of staff and distribution of materials. This sector of the hospitality industry faces the unique challenge of feeding people while they are travelling between destinations. There are therefore some challenges to overcome.

- The mode of transport needs to be designed in such a way as to enable food service to take place. On board aircraft space is very limited so that galleys are kept as small as possible. On the railways and on-board ships, there is more space so that kitchen layouts more closely resemble the production areas found in more conventional surroundings.
- There may be significant logistics problems in terms of effectively supplying 'outlets' that do not always directly return to their point of origin. This necessitates setting-up a complex supply chain that enables aircraft, trains, cars and ships to be provisioned in a number of different ways at different stages of their route.
- Food and drink are not the sole or even the main reason for the customer purchase, they are simply a part of the travel package. Such packages are often based on a combination of price and time of departure and/or arrival and not on the quality of food served. However, if the food service standard is unsatisfactory, despite its low level of importance in the purchase decision, it can cause high levels of customer dissatisfaction. Food service providers need to be aware both of the marketing and of the operational implications of this.

Airline

One of the unique aspects of airline catering is that the cost of the catering service is usually included in the price of the airline ticket. The market for in-flight meals is closely related to the growth in the number of people travelling by air. However, the nature of in-flight catering is changing because of marketing, financial and operational pressures on airlines. Some airlines have chosen to compete on the basis of low cost and the fact that passengers need a simple and efficient journey from airport to airport. Some airlines have even opted for virtually no cabin service at all on short-haul flights. In contrast, on many long-haul flights, airlines often choose the quality of their food and service as a way of differentiating themselves from the competition.

Some airlines reduce cabin service to a simple cold snack, a trolley buffet or the provision of buffet in the departure lounge to allow passengers to select their requirements for the journey. Operating procedures are divided into production, transportation to the airport, the loading of materials on the aircraft, the service of waste for washing back to the production unit.

Rail

The type of catering facility a passenger can expect when travelling by rail may be viewed from two perspectives: in-terminal catering and on-board catering. This is dependent on the duration of journey, class of ticket purchased and the time of the day. On-board catering can range from a beverage served from a trolley to a silver-served three or four course meal in a Pullman car. Prior to any catering service, there is a complex system of ordering food items to be done. On UK Intercity East Coast this is done weekly using a computerised system where passenger numbers are calculated and orders are made a week in advance for each train. Whereas in the restaurant car, operating the express diner, first class Pullman menus, most menu items are prepared using the conventional cooking methods as far as possible with food being brought on board raw.

The types of service offered on board include; trolley service, buffet bar, restaurant car, Pullman service and sleeper service. There are a number of problems which are inherent in the provision of food and beverage on trains aside from the fact that the kitchen is moving at high speed. Water, refrigeration and electricity supplies are expensive and revenue losses can be costly if they fail. In order to achieve the high standards of service, staffing levels must also be high.

Additionally, timetabling has to be accurate so that staff are not away from their home depot overnight, yet providing enough staff to deal with a busy service.

Sea

The classification of commercial catering within marine travel encompasses two distinct sectors – passengers on short sea routes and clientele on board cruise ships for an extended duration of five days or more. There is generally catering provided at the port terminus.

The number and types of catering facilities on board ferries vary according to the physical constraints of the vessel, the amount and type of passengers it carries and the duration of the journey. Food and beverage provided in outlets ranging from kiosks for simple snacks to self-service style restaurants to silver-service restaurants to ever fast food. Computerised central purchasing is common practice given the scale of the operations. However, in keeping with customer demand for freshly produced food, cook-chill production systems are also incorporated, with regeneration of dishes on board ship, while other food items, especially fast food products are prepared at their shore-based counterparts.

B3 By pooling their resources, some smaller hotel groups hope to confront the rapid advances of the multinational hotel companies whose financial and marketing power could, over the long term, threaten their survival.

Multinational American and European hotel groups are looking into the prospects of expanding their brands across the Asia-Pacific region through a variety of options: franchise, management, marketing, reservations or even equity.

Many Asia-Pacific hotels owned by property companies hit by the economic crisis are being gradually offloaded to international investors who will invariably turn them over to the global groups to run, which will place further competitive pressure on the local and regional groups.

Many small- and medium-sized hotel groups are facing competition from big-league hotel chains and, as a result, could join a consortium as an additional source of international business, marketing and networking.

The role of the multinational companies is significant with their increasing contribution to the economy. In the hospitality industry, average room rate (ARR) and occupancy are the two most critical factors that determine profitability, since most of the marginal revenue gets added to the bottom-line. ARR in turn depends upon location, brand image, star rating, quality of facilities, pricing of value added services, complementary services offered and the seasonal factor.

When hotels are affiliated to an international hotel chain the benefit can be mutual. The tie-up puts the hotel on the global map with access to the chain's reservation network worldwide. For the international hotel chain they can ride on the boom of the industry without making enormous capital investments on infrastructure and facilities. Associations with international brand also play a major role in image building and attracting foreign tourists.

However, the value of the international brand gets diluted if a foreign entity enters an agreement with several companies. So the role of multinational chains/groups of hotels in the hospitality industry and their contribution to the economy is significant.

Positive contributions to the international hospitality industry made by the emergence of multinational hotel groups:

- Creates competitions in the hospitality industry thus encourage hotels to strive better.
- The emergence of multinational hotel groups might cause the hospitality industry to grow.
- People might travel to more exotic places if hotels are available there.
- People travelling more often creates more business for the airline industry.
- Creates more jobs for the hospitality industry.

Negative contributions to the international hospitality industry made by the emergence of multinational hotel groups:

- Competition might result in the small or individual establishment losing a share in the industry and end up disappearing altogether.
- A change in the current trend causes certain establishment to reduce its size.
- Areas cleared for these hotels brings unhappy people creating political problems, affecting the hospitality industry.
- The multinational hotel groups might just 'eat up' the smaller hotel establishments.
- The competition might be between the multinational hotel groups and larger hotel groups resulting in the smaller establishments having 'no stand' in the industry.
- Those establishments that do not meet the service standard will be out of the industry.
- These multinational hotel groups might grow and dominate the hospitality industry one day.

B4 Student's answers to cover some of the following.

(a) Contract catering is where there is an agreement to provide food and beverage for a specific period for an agreed fee.

Contract catering companies have diversified into hotel services and facilities management (including cleaning, security, and maintenance), which has proved both lucrative and profitable. Contract catering (and the other aforementioned contractible services on offer) is essentially employed to provide practical and cost effective solutions for the management of non-core activities of the [client] company. For example employers providing a staff canteen and instead of managing the facility themselves, they contract professionals to do it for them

Major markets are healthcare, business, industry, military, prisons and transportation; it is dominated by a few large sophisticated global firms although there are many smaller niche players.

(b)
- By looking at the feedback of food quality
- Monitoring service provided to ensure customer satisfaction
- Ensuring reasonable price being set for food and beverage
- Maintenance of equipment for longer durability

(c) Management fee (sometimes called 'cost plus'), fixed cost, full cost recovery (nil cost), commercial return, guaranteed performance

Cost plus management fee – The client or institution pays the actual cost of the food, supplies, labour and other direct costs plus a management fee. These fees are typically based on a percentage of managed volume. The institution assumes all of the risk but has a higher level of control over the service.

Fixed price contract – Is less popular with contractors as they have to accurately assess all the catering costs for the period ahead and then bill clients with one-twelfth of the year's projected costs each month.

Profit and loss – In this style of arrangement, the managed services provider collects all revenues and/or invoices for services at a predetermined rate per person. It covers all operating costs and retains the resulting profits. Some agreements include the payment of a commission or rent back to the client. The ability to pay commission or rent is based on having sufficient volume to cover fixed operating costs & generating sufficient funds after variable costs to earn a reasonable profit with funds left over for commission or rent. In a profit or loss contract the operator assumes greater risks but also gains the right to upside profits.

Partnership agreements – the client and the contract caterer share risks, rewards and control. They work together investing in facilities, attracting customers, and building demand, sharing the costs and sharing in the upside profits.

B5 (a) Budget hotels are generally good-quality, value-for-money, bedrooms designed and marketed in such a way as to appeal to the travelling public.

- Lower tariffs than industry norms
- 2/3 star standard of accommodation
- Limited facilities and services
- Aimed at the transient market
- Located on major road networks or in secondary urban locations (retail parks)
- Catering is usually provided by an adjacent food operation
- Purpose built in terms of location and design
- Standardised operational procedures and charges nationwide
- Branded network of hotels

(b) The prosperous years of the late 1980s facilitated rapid growth in provision. However 3-, 4- and 5-star hotels suffered due to the economic recession at the turn of the decade, the budget sector flourished with demand out-stripping supply. Conditions of economic stringency seemed to have less impact on the budget sector. Indeed the economic necessity of 'trading down' from high tariff hotels could actually have benefited budget hotels. This point should not be over emphasised since the building of new budget bedroom blocks did slow during the difficult 1990–93 trading period.

In the USA franchising of budget hotel concepts are big businesses with franchises continuously being sought by franchisors. It is likely that with the involvement of foreign hotel groups that franchise agreements will become as common in the UK as they are in their home countries.

(c) The correct location is the key to the success of a budget hotel. It must be situated in a place with easy access. Adequate car parking space is important. Land and planning permission must be available at the right price. These criteria therefore limit the choice of sites available to potential developers and operators. Budget accommodation cannot be provided economically on premium priced land, for example city-centre locations are off-limits due to the price of the land, therefore budget hotel are forced into out-of town, secondary urban locations on main trunk roads.

This fits in well with recent building developments in the form of retail and leisure parks in out-of-town locations and many new retail developments include planning for a budget hotel.

BIBLIOGRAPHY

BIBLIOGRAPHY

The following key text books have been consulted in the preparation of this Study Guide, and referred to (where relevant) in the text.

Beirman, D (Oct 15th, 2008) *Tourism and the Global Economic Crisis of 2008*, (accessed 10th September, 2009) (http://www.eturbonews.com/5604/tourism-and-global-economic-crisis-2008).

Brotherton, B (2003) *The International Hospitality Industry 'Structure, Characteristics and Issues*, Oxford: Butterworth-Heinemann.

Campbell Smith, G (1967) '*Marketing the Meal Experience*', Guildford: University of Surrey.

Cooper, C; Fletcher, J; Fyall, A; Gilbert, D; Wanhill, S (2005) *Tourism: Principles and Practice*, (3rd Edition), Harlow, Essex: Pearson Education Limited

Dale, G (2005) *Travel and Tourism,* (BTEC National Book 1), Oxford: Heinemann Educational Publishers.

de Kadt, E (1979) *Tourism: Passport to Development?*, Oxford University Press, New York.

Doxey, G V (1975) 'When enough's enough: the natives are restless in Old Niagara', Heritage Canada 2 (2), 26-7

Foskett, D; Ceserani, V; Kinton, R *'The Theory of Catering'* (10th Edition), Abingdon: Hodder and Stoughton.

Holloway, C (2006) *The Business of Tourism*, (7th edition), Harlow, Essex: Pearson Education Limited.

Johnson, G; Scholes, K and Whittington, R (2008) *Exploring Corporate Strategy,* (8th Edition), Harlow, Essex: Pearson Education Ltd.

Jones, P (1988) *Foodservice Operations,* (2nd Edition), London: Cassell.

Jones, P (1996) *Introduction to Hospitality Operations 'An Indispensable Guide to the Industry',* London: Cassell.

Jones, P (ed.) (2002) *Introduction to Hospitality Operations: An Indispensable Guide to the Industry* (2nd Edition), London: Continuum.

Knowles, T (1994) *Hospitality Management 'An Introduction',* Harlow, Essex: Addison Wesley Longman Limited.

Kotler, P; Bowen, J and Makens, J C (2006) *Marketing for Tourism and Hospitality,* (4th edition), New Jersey: Pearson Education Inc.

Litteljohn, D (2003) *Hotels: The International Hospitality Industry: Structure, Characteristics and Issues,* Oxford: Butterworth-Heinemann.

Page, S J and Connell, J (2006) *Tourism: A Modern Synthesis,* (2nd edition), London: Thomson Learning.

Poon, A (1998) 'All-inclusive resorts', *Travel and Tourism Analyst*, 6:62-77.

INDEX